Healthy Baby Food

Nirelle Tolstoshev

NEW HOLLAND

The Tolstoshev family.

This book is dedicated to Hugo Benjamin
and Alexander George Tolstoshev
who provided the inspiration for the creation of this book

healthy baby contents

introduction
Page 10

dietitian's note
Page 13

good nutrition
Page 14

healthy baby kitchen
Page 18

four to eight months
Page 23

Apple Puree
Apple and rice cereal
Avocado Puree
Banana Puree
Pumpkin Puree
Pumpkin and rice cereal
Broccoli Puree
Red lentil Puree
Combination Ideas

twelve to eighteen months
Page 45

Second pasta bolognese
Scrambled eggs with ricotta and parsley
Ham, vegetables and rice
Gnocchi with broccoli and chicken
Gnocchi with pumpkin and corn
Vegetable lasagne
Egg and bread crumbs
Ham and vegetable frittata
Apricot chicken rice
Boston (baked) beans
Pasta with vegetable sauce
Ham and vegetable ratatouille
Brown lentils with ham
Sausages and pasta
Cheesy maccaroni

eight to twelve months
Page 31

Pumpkin, yoghurt and cous cous
Chicken and corn
Lentil, pasta and vegetables
Chicken, red lentils and pasta
Sweet potato rice
Beef and sweet potato
First pasta bolognese
Polenta and vegetables
Beef and spinach
Hokkien noodles with chicken and vegetables
Cous cous salad
Eggplant, sweet potato and cous cous

eighteen to twenty four months
Page 63

finger foods
Page 87

Chicken and mushroom quiche
Shepherds pie
Fried rice with egg
Chicken and pea risotto
Scrambled tomato eggs
Pasta with pork
Roast pork with gravy
Lasagne
Chicken and vegetable soup
Sweet and sour pork
Fish and vegetables
Ham and zucchini (courgette) soup
Tuna pasta bake
Chicken and vegetable cous cous
Braised steak and bread pies
Meatballs
Chicken pasta bake
Potato and leek soup
Chicken and bacon slow cook
Chicken noodles with vegetables
Beef stroganoff
Mexican wraps

Sandwich ideas
Spinach and cheese pie
Pasta cakes
Lamb kebabs
Chicken and vegetable scrolls
Roast lamb patties
Spring rolls
Pasty slice
Toddler pizza
Flat bread toasties
Chicken and vegetable rolls
Ham and vegetable slice
Pumpkin and cheese balls
Roast vegetable medley
Chicken croquettes
Tuna patties
Beef rissoles
Pumpkin and bean squares
Schnitzel fingers
Toast ideas
Ham and polenta squares
Pea and corn fritters
Bacon and banana toast
Fish fingers
Chicken and broccoli pies

snacks
Page 115

Cereal bars
Fruit salad
Weetbix slice
Ham and corn muffins
Date mini-scones
Cheese and vegemite pastries
Pumpkin tarts
Banana mini-muffins
Sweet potato chips
French toast crusts
Weetbix cookies
Rice bubble slice
Jam pin wheels
Cheese biscuits

sweeties
Page 131

Custard and fruit
Mango rice pudding
Bread and fruit pudding
Fruit crumble
Strawberry pikelets
Berry sago
Pineapple pastries
Caramel bananas
Apple pie
Stewed rhubarb
Banana rice cream
Baked apples with yoghurt

fussy eaters
Page 145

index
Page 153

INTRODUCTION

Congratulations! You are the proud owner of a little tiny person. Did anyone mention to you that there is no user manual to consult? Babies provide so much joy, and you will be constantly amazed by every little thing that your baby does. The joyous moments will be balanced by the myriad of challenges that your baby will present you with, one of which is eating food. Babies have needs that are similar to adults in this area, they will grumble when they are hungry, and will be more cheerful and content when they are given a nutritious range of interesting and hunger satisfying foods.

I speak from experience, having raised twin boys, who are now two years old. I spent a lot of time trying out different food types with my boys, some that were popular, and others that were hurled around the room in protest.

This book represents a collection of recipe ideas that I found useful to achieve the following:

1. To prepare nutritious, balanced meals for babies aged 0-2 years.
2. To teach babies about a wide range of foods, preparing them to be adventurous eaters as toddlers.
3. To prepare simple recipes based on widely available ingredients that can be gathered from your local supermarket.
4. To provide meals with quick preparation time, allowing more time for cuddles and play and less time in the kitchen.

It is my hope that after using this book for a short time you will gain the confidence and knowledge to experiment with different ingredients and meal ideas yourself. The recipes in this book for children aged twelve months and over can be enjoyed throughout the toddler years, and indeed by the whole family.

You will need to decide when to start solids, with the help of your doctor, nurse or other health professionals. This will usually be somewhere from four months onwards which is where this book starts.

This book has been structured into the sequential stages your baby will go through, starting from first solids and moving through to increased texture, flavour and variety. Some babies will progress through the stages quicker than others, and this can be due to the number of teeth they have, their ability to chew more complex foods and their general development level. Do not rush your baby through the stages, rather let them tell you when they are ready to progress.

It is my reccomendation that once your baby starts solids, you stock your kitchen well (refer to the following section), plan meals ahead of time, cook several portions at a time and freeze meals. This approach will make your life easier and ensure your baby has a constant supply of varied, delicious and nutritious food.

You will be lucky if you don't encounter a fussy eater in your household. I have dedicated a section to fussy eaters at the back of this book should the need arise.

I hope you enjoy meal times with your baby. Treasure this time as it is just so special. Happy cooking.

Dietitian's Note

As a dietitian and mum of two girls, it was a pleasure to be asked to review and contribute to this book.

Healthy family eating is a passion of mine. Family meals are important rituals, there is evidence that when children eat with their family they have better nutrition and better communication skills. Kids that eat with their families also do better at school and tend to get in less trouble with drugs and alcohol. So you can see there is more than just eating going on.

For many people the first time they consider cooking on a regular basis is when they have children. Starting solids might be a catalyst for refreshing or improving your cooking skills and organising your kitchen.

This very useful book will help you do these things. You will find easy to follow recipes with good quality basic ingredients. Healthy eating isn't as hard as we are often led to believe. Cooking for and with your family is a great start to a life time of good nutrition. I wish you all the best with feeding your healthy baby.

Susan Williams

Accredited Practising Dietitian /
Accredited Nutritionist
Zest Nutrition Consulting, NSW, Australia

 = LOW SALT

 = GLUTEN FREE

 = LOW SUGAR

 = LOW FAT

 = NO ADDED SALT

 = NO ADDED SUGAR

Good nutrition starts at birth

It is good parenting to take the time to prepare and offer nutritious food for your baby. A healthy diet rich in nutrients (vitamins and minerals) and a balanced range of grains, vegetables, fruit, dairy and meat (or meat alternative) is really important for babies, and there are several reasons why:

1. Babies, on average triple their weight in their first year, and they need a lot of nutrients to keep up with such rapid growth and development.

2. Many different nutrients are required to strengthen the immune system to fight diseases, or lessen the effects of illnesses they encounter as babies and toddlers.

3. A well-balanced diet helps babies develop their cognitive and social skills. These are the skills that help babies crawl, roll, walk, hold small objects and move around, and also interact and socialise with other babies and people.

4. A nutritious diet early in life is habit forming to minimise the risk of developing diet related diseases later in life, such as obesity, type 2 diabetes and some cancers.

Important nutrients needed include iron and vitamin c, along with an enormous list of others. The table on the following page gives a guide to foods rich in each nutrient, and the role of each vitamin or mineral in the body. With a balanced diet, babies do not need vitamin or mineral supplements, unless they have certain medical conditions, are born prematurely or have been advised to under medical supervision. Importantly, by giving your baby a varied diet of different healthy foods, you will be ensuring each of these daily requirements is met. The recipes in this book enable you to do this, ensuring that your babies little body is growing and developing to its full potential.

You do not need to give your baby low fat versions of foods such as milk and yoghurt, unless instructed to do so by your health care provider and this is because there are many vitamins that are soluble in fat, such as Vitamins A, D, E and K. Small children have high energy requirements and only small stomach capacity so healthy fats are essential in meeting their energy needs. It is important that fats come from quality, nutritious foods like fish, avocado, dairy, seeds and nuts (and their oils) and not non nutritious foods like fast foods cooked in saturated fat.

Babies should be introduced to salt and sugar very slowly, and this is so that they can get used to a variety of foods without the distraction of salt and sugar to artificially flavour their food. Where possible avoid adding salt to babies food, when using bought sauces, pastes and canned foods choose "no added salt" varieties. This is because babies and young childrens kidneys can't cope with a lot of salt. Salty foods like bacon, ham, cheese, vegemite and full salt commercial foods should only be given in small quantities. The recipes in this book are all low sugar and include low salt stock and tomato paste. If you don't have the low salt versions on hand, use less than half the amount.

Fluid intake is very important for babies to remain hydrated amid the flurry of daily activity. Balance fluid intake from breastmilk and/or formula with small amounts of water throughout the day, in increasing amounts as formula or breastfeeding decreases over time.

Nutritional icons are included for each recipe, displaying those low in fat, salt and sugar, and those that are gluten free. Gluten free recipes assume that you will use gluten free pastes and stocks. Naturally, you can use gluten free pasta and make some of the recipes that are not marked as gluten free.

VITAMIN / MINERAL	SOURCES	ROLE
Iron	Red meat, chicken, iron-fortified rice cereal	Red blood cell turnover, brain growth
Vitamin C	Oranges, mandarins, kiwifruit, strawberries, broccoli, capsicum (pepper)	Healthy skin, hair and teeth, red blood cell growth, immune function
Calcium	Milk, cheese, yoghurt, soy milk, tofu, lentils, chickpeas, broccoli, salmon, raisins, parsley	Bone growth, nerve function, muscle contraction, healthy teeth
Folate	Green leafy vegetables such as spinach and broccoli, avocado, oranges, mandarins, beans, folate enriched foods	Blood and brain function, overall growth
Vitamin A	Sweet potato, carrot, tomatoes, green leafy vegetables such as spinach, broccoli	Skin, bone and teeth growth, mucous membrane function, vision
B Group Vitamins	Meat, potatoes, bananas, lentils, beans, tuna	Heart and brain growth, nerve function, digestion and food metabolism, healthy skin, nails and hair
Vitamin E	Seeds, nuts and grains, green leafy vegetables such as spinach, broccoli	Red blood cell metabolism, antioxidant
Vitamin D	Seeds, oily fish, butter, exposure to sunlight	Important for calcium absorption, bone growth
Vitamin K	Green leafy vegetables such as spinach, broccoli, lettuce and spring onions	Blood clotting, bone metabolism, kidney function
Magnesium	Nuts, seeds, grains, beans, green leafy vegetables such as spinach	Muscle and nerve function, heart rhythm, healthy immune system, blood sugar regulation, bone metabolism
Phosphorous	Seeds, meat, fish, cheese soy products, whole grains, brazil nuts	Energy production, cell division, bone and teeth growth
Potassium	Root vegetables such as potato and parsnip, lima beans, banana, avocado, dried fruit	Heart function, blood pressure, fluid balance, nerve and kidney function
Selenium	Brazil nuts, walnuts, tuna, eggs, beef, chicken, corn, wheat, rice	Protein function, antioxidant, thyroid and immune function
Zinc	Meat, shellfish, dairy, cereal foods	Immune and thyroid function, growth and repair of tissue, digestion

Adapted from 1. *Essentials of Human Nutrition*, Third Edition 2007, University of Oxford, Edited by Mann, J. & Truswell, A.S, Oxford University Press. AND 2. *Understanding Normal and Clinical Nutrition*, Seventh Edition, 2006 Rolfer, Pinner & Whitney, Thomson Wadsworth and in consultation with Susan Williams, Zest Nutrition Consulting, NSW, Australia.

healthy baby kitchen

Setting up your kitchen

Having a well stocked kitchen makes cooking for your baby easier.

The following list includes most of the staple ingredients used in the recipes in this book.

All of these ingredients are available in your local supermarket and can be stocked in your pantry, cupboard or freezer ahead of time.

With a little bit of planning, you can simply buy the fresh ingredients for the recipe you choose, making shopping and cooking even easier.

Stock your pantry with...

Beans - canned
Kidney beans aswell as mixed beans are useful in casseroles and for boston beans.

Breadcrumbs
Basic breadcrumbs are handy for crumbing food to be eaten as finger food, and can be used to add to dishes to thicken or add texture.

Corn - canned
Creamed corn is a great first solid for babies, and also makes a great addition to many dishes to provide natural sweetness and texture.
Canned corn kernels are worth having on hand as a nutritious addition to almost any savoury dish.

Cous cous
Cous cous is usually located with the dried pasta and is great as a first texture, following acceptance of fruit and vegetable purees.

Dried herbs
Start adding herbs to your babies meals early, as a way of adding flavour without salt once purees are tolerated. Dried Italian herbs, mixed herbs and dried parsley are great options.

Fruit
Fruit in cans and plastic containers, such as peaches, pears and berries are good alternatives to fresh fruit, and can be eaten cold, with yoghurt or added to deserts.

Flour
Plain, self raising and rice flour are all used in this book, and are handy to have in your pantry.

Honey
Honey is a great natural sweetener for baby meals, but should only be given to babies over one year due to the extremely rare risk of bacterial blood poisoning.

Noodles

Dried noodles are handy for asian stir fry dishes.

Olive Oil

The addition of oil to baby meals should be avoided where possible. If required olive oil is a good option. Olive oil spray can be used to minimise the amount of oil being added.

Pasta

Small pasta is great as a first texture, following acceptance of fruit and vegetable purees. Soup pasta and short angel hair are good early options for babies. Larger pasta shapes such as penne, shells and spiral are great as finger food, with or without sauces.

Lentils

Dried red lentils, available in supermarkets, are fast cooking and very nutritious for babies. Canned brown lentils are also worth having on hand.

Stock your pantry with....

Polenta
Polenta is available in supermarkets, usually with the dried pasta and is an easy, quick option mixed with meat and vegetables.

Rice
Brown and white rice are useful to have on hand. Consider the precooked varieties, although a little more expensive, they can be more convenient when you are time poor.

Rolled Oats
Oats are great as porridge with honey or fruit for breakfast, and are handy for adding as crumble toppings.

Sago
Sago, similar to tapioca, is a tiny pearl shape starch, originally from palm trees, and is an inexpensive option for soft puddings for babies. Sago is usually found with the desserts such as canned rice cream in the supermarket.

Stock
Beef and chicken stock add extra flavour to baby meals, and options available include reduced salt and gluten free.

Tomato paste (puree)
Tomato paste adds extra flavour to dishes, and options available in the supermarket include low salt and herb pastes all available in different size sachets and tubs.

Tuna - canned
Tuna is popular with babies in pastas, patties and mornays.

Weet-bix
Weet-bix makes a great warm breakfast for babies, with fruit or honey added. It also makes a good base for snacks.

Stock your freezer with...

Berries
Frozen berries are a convenient alternative to fresh berries, for adding to weetbix, porridge and desert recipes.

Pastry
Shortcrust pastry is handy for pies and quiche.
Filo pastry is used for pies and pastries.
Puff pastry is used for sausage rolls, scrolls and pastries.

Peas and Beans
Frozen peas and beans provide nutrition, colour and texture to baby meals, and are convenient additions to many dishes.

Spinach
Frozen spinach is convenient and nutritious for babies, and can be found packaged in easy to use cubes.

healthy baby
four to eight months

healthy baby four to eight months

This section starts by introducing your baby to a variety of single fruit and vegetable purees. Each food must be trialled on its own initially, as, in the unlikely event that your baby has an allergic reaction, you will then know which food has caused it. Once your baby is familiar with individual flavours, it is time to combine foods for more interesting flavour.

In addition to fruit and vegetable purees, baby rice cereal is a great first solid, and once your baby has tolerated it, it can be mixed with fruit or vegetable purees. Iron fortified rice cereal is available in your supermarket and comes on its own or with dried fruit (e.g. banana) for flavour. At this stage, meat is generally not recommended for babies, so this section covers fruit and vegetables, and the next section includes the introduction of meat. The basic rule of thumb is to steam the chopped vegetable or fruit, adding a small amount of water, formula or breast milk, then puree and offer each food individually, over several feeds. Mixing purees with breast milk or formula can make them taste more familiar to your baby, otherwise water works just as well, and will be used in these recipes. Purees will keep in the fridge for four days in a sealed container and can be frozen for several months. There are ice cube trays on the market designed to be easy to empty, and I would recommend cooking batches ahead of time, then popping the cubes into containers ready to go when you need them. A hand held mixer is easiest, try to borrow one if you don't have one, as you will only need it for a matter of months. If you are really stuck, a fork, or potato masher will get you by. You will need a saucepan with a steamer that sits on top, and these are available at most large supermarkets. Fruits like apples and pears, along with vegetables like pumpkin, zucchini, sweet potato, carrot, broccoli and potato need

to be cooked before pureeing. Banana and avocado can be pureed without cooking, and these foods can be really helpful when you are travelling, shopping or not near a kitchen.

I haven't provided a recipe for steaming and pureeing every individual food, as the formula is similar for all. Rather, I will show you how to puree some fruits and some vegetables, and then how to combine flavours, and to combine with baby rice cereal.

Baby plastic teaspoons are available from the supermarket and initially, your baby may only take one or two teaspoons. Your baby will slowly build an appetite to accept more food, more often. As a guide, you may want to give your baby new flavours at lunchtime in the first instance. This allows you to monitor for allergic reactions during the day, rather than overnight. Allergic reactions are extremely rare; please consult your doctor or paediatrician if you have any concerns.

Stick with one flavour for several consecutive feeds, rather than challenging them with many flavours in one day, so that they have time to get to know the flavour. It may take several attempts for your baby to accept a food, so keep trying and don't assume that if they don't like it initially that they won't like it eventually.

Once the lunch time feed is tolerated, slowly move to three solid meals a day, this may take several weeks.

Apple puree

Apples make a good choice for babies.
This recipe can used to make apricot, peach or pear puree.

4 apples, peeled and sliced   Water

Steam apples on stove until very soft.
Add a small amount of water and puree until soft and thick.

8 serves

Apple and rice cereal

Any fruit puree can be combined with rice cereal in this way.

1 tablespoon / 20g apple puree

1 teaspoon / 5g baby rice cereal

Water

Combine ingredients above and mix with a spoon to a thick texture.

1 serve

Avocado puree

Avocado is very convenient as it does not require cooking and is delicious mixed with mashed banana. Avocado puree can be stored in the fridge for four days, but does not freeze well.

½ small avocado

Cut avocado in half, remove seed and skin and mash with a fork until smooth. Add water if required

4 serves

DIETITIAN'S TIP

The delicious creamy taste of avocado is due to the high level of healthy mono unsaturated fat. Avocadoes are extremely nutritious, providing vitamin E, Potassium and Niacin, they are filling and an ideal replacement for butter on sandwiches.

Banana puree

Banana is very nutritious and convenient as it does not require cooking and is delicious mixed with avocado. Banana puree can be stored in the fridge for four days, but does not freeze well.

1 banana

Peel banana and mash with a fork until smooth.

2 serves

Pumpkin puree

This recipe can be followed to puree sweet potato, potato, carrot, corn (remove from cob), eggplant or parsnip.

¼ small pumpkin, peeled and chopped   Water

Steam pumpkin on stovetop until soft when pricked with a fork.
Puree, adding some of the cooking water to form a thick texture.

6 serves

Pumpkin and rice cereal

Use this recipe with other vegetables alone or in combination.

1 tablespoon /20g mashed pumpkin   1 teaspoon / 5g baby rice cereal   Water

Combine ingredients above and mix with a spoon to a thick texture.

1 serve

Broccoli puree

Green vegetables are important in your babies diet, and should be included from the start. This recipe can be followed for zucchini (courgette), green bean, cauliflower or peas.

½ head of broccoli, chopped   Water

Steam broccoli on stovetop until soft when pricked with a fork.
Puree to a thick texture.

6 serves

Red lentil puree

Red lentils are highly nutritious, convenient to store and easy and quick to cook.

½ cup / 70g / 2.5oz dry red lentils
Water

Place lentils in a saucepan and cover with water. Bring to the boil, then simmer for five to ten minutes, or until lentils are soft.
Check often and add extra water if required.
Remove from heat and puree.

4 serves

four to eight months

Combination ideas

Here are some ideas for combining flavours (combine equal parts) for your baby, once he or she has tolerated individual foods. Once you have tried some of these, you will have a feel for how to combine three, four and more flavours to provide nutrition and flavour for your baby. Rice cereal can be added to any of these combinations for a meal that may keep your baby full for longer. Yoghurt is a healthy addition to purees, and can be eaten on its own too.

Pumpkin and broccoli
Carrot and potato
Pumpkin and apple
Sweet potato and cauliflower
Sweet potato and corn

Corn and green beans
Avocado and banana
Apple and pear
Apple, pumpkin and zucchini
Apple, carrot and potato

healthy baby
eight to twelve months

healthy baby
eight to twelve months

During this stage your baby will be ready to try meat such as chicken and beef, and these foods can be introduced slowly over the next few months.

Also, your baby will be ready for some interesting textural foods, such as cous cous, rice and pasta, and these should be introduced very slowly. If the change in texture is too dramatic, you may end up wearing the meal!

Very simple finger food such as small pieces of cracker biscuit or pieces of steamed, soft vegetables can also be introduced during the next few months. If your baby progresses quickly, and is looking for more finger foods, particularly if they have several teeth, then start making recipes from the finger foods section of this book.

This section involves more combinations of flavours than the last section, with limited addition of salt, stock, tomato paste or sugar.

As your baby develops, and throughout this section, try to slowly limit the degree that you puree the food so that they get used to the change in texture.

These recipes produce several portions, and can be stored in the fridge for four days, or frozen in air tight containers in the freezer for several months.
I recommend making two recipes, a day apart, so that your baby has some variety, for a couple of days. By the time you have made each of these recipes a couple of times, you should be ready to move onto the next section.

Your baby will accept most food at this age, however if you encounter a fussy eater, please refer to the later section in this book.

In addition to the recipes outlined here, also consider weetbix or rolled oats (porridge) mixed with formula, milk or breast milk and fruit for a healthy and nutritious breakfast.

Pumpkin, yoghurt and cous cous

As you make this a few times, you can increase the amount of cous cous versus the pumpkin. You can also try adding cooked chicken or beef to this recipe.

1 cup / 250g / 8oz cooked mashed pumpkin

1 tablespoon / 15g / .5oz cous cous

¼ cup / 60g / 2oz natural yoghurt

Place cous cous in a bowl and cover with water. Microwave for twenty seconds, then cover and stand for one minute. Combine cous cous with pumpkin and yoghurt.

4 serves

eight to twelve months

Chicken and corn

Once you have tried this recipe, consider adding other vegetables, and yoghurt or rice cereal.

100g / 3.5oz preservative free chicken mince

125g / 4oz can creamed corn

Cook chicken mince in frypan, adding water to avoid sticking.
Add creamed corn until warmed through and puree if required.

4 serves

Lentils pasta and vegetables

¼ small butternut pumpkin, cubed

1 large carrot cubed

1 zucchini (courgette), cubed

Handful green beans, chopped finely

¼ cup / 35g / 1.0oz red lentils

½ cup / 60g / 2oz small pasta

500ml / 16fl oz low salt chicken stock, or water if you prefer

2 tablespoons / 40g / 1fl oz ricotta or natural yoghurt

Place all ingredients except for yoghurt or ricotta in slow cooker or saucepan. For slow cooker, simmer for two hours. For saucepan, simmer for thirty minutes or until lentils are soft. Puree to desired consistency, adding extra water if required. Stir in ricotta or yoghurt before serving.

8 serves

Chicken, red lentils and pasta

200g / 7oz chicken mince (ground meat)
½ cup / 70g / 2oz red lentils
½ cup / 60g / 2oz small pasta
½ cup / 125ml water

DIETITIAN'S TIP

Lentils are a great source of protein, carbohydrate, zinc, potassium and fibre. Red lentils are so easy to prepare, as they don't need to be pre-soaked.

Put ingredients in to saucepan and simmer for thirty to forty minutes or until lentils are soft, adding more water if required. Puree to desired consistency.

8 serves

Sweet potato rice

To cook the rice:
A half of a cup or rice, microwaved with a cup of water gives one cup of cooked rice.

1 cup / 250g / 8oz cooked and mashed sweet potato

1 cup / 250g / 8oz cooked rice

2 tablespoons / 40g / 1.5oz yoghurt

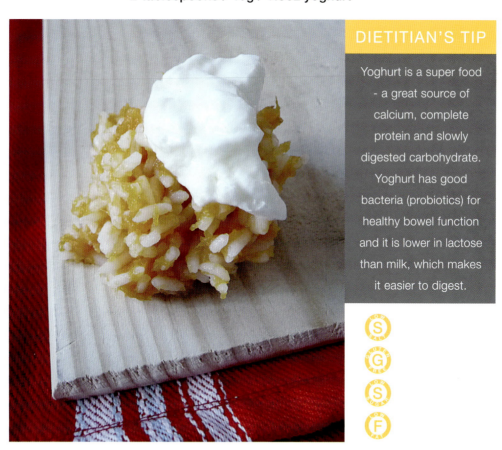

DIETITIAN'S TIP

Yoghurt is a super food - a great source of calcium, complete protein and slowly digested carbohydrate. Yoghurt has good bacteria (probiotics) for healthy bowel function and it is lower in lactose than milk, which makes it easier to digest.

Combine all ingredients, and puree if necessary, to desired consistency.

8 serves

Beef and sweet potato

Consider adding other vegetables to this recipe, and also adding yoghurt or rice cereal.

100g / 3.5oz beef mince (ground meat)

1 cup / 250g / 8oz sweet potato, cooked and mashed

Cook beef mince in frypan, adding water to avoid sticking.

Add mashed sweet potato until combined.

4 serves

First pasta bolognese

(Second pasta bolognese follows in the next section)

200g / 7oz mince meat (ground meat)

1 large carrot, grated

½ cup / 60g / 2oz uncooked small soup pasta

200g / 7oz canned or fresh diced tomatoes

Handful of grated cheese

Cook mince in frypan, adding water to avoid sticking. Add grated carrot and tomatoes, and simmer for twenty minutes, or until carrots are soft.

Cook tiny pasta in water until very soft, then strain.

Stir pasta into sauce with cheese. Puree to preferred consistency.

8 serves

Polenta and vegetables

½ red capsicum (bell pepper), diced

1 cup / 250g / 8oz pumpkin, grated

50g / 1.8oz frozen spinach cube

½ cup / 90g / 3oz dry polenta

2 cups / 500ml / 16fl oz water

Handful grated cheese

Place water and polenta into a saucepan and stir on medium heat for two minutes, or until soft. Cook pumpkin and capsicum on medium heat in a frypan, adding water to avoid sticking. Add spinach after a couple of minutes, then spoon polenta in with vegetables. Add cheese and serve.

6 serves

Beef and spinach

200g / 7oz beef mince (ground meat)

3 large handfuls of chopped spinach

1 medium size potato, peeled and chopped

125g / 4oz can creamed corn

Handful grated cheese

Cook mince in frypan, adding water to avoid sticking.

Boil potatoes until soft, and at the last second add sliced spinach to wilt.

Puree potato and spinach,

combine with mince and then add creamed corn. Sprinkle in cheese.

6 serves

Hokkien noodles with chicken & vegetables

If your baby has not had hokkein noodles before, give them as finger food initially (ie. the day before) to ensure tolerance.

150g / 5oz preservative free fresh hokkein noodles
100g / 3.5oz chicken mince (ground meat)
1 carrot, finely grated
Handful chopped mint (optional)
1 cup / 175g / 6oz chopped bok choy, broccoli or peas

Place noodles in large bowl of hot water to separate. Cook chicken mince in large frypan adding water to avoid sticking. Add carrot, mint and green vegetables and cook until soft. Drain noodles, chop into smaller pieces and add to pan. Partially or completely puree to your babies liking, adding water if required.

6 serves

Cous cous salad

This is a dish served cold, and is great for a hot summer day. Some recommendations suggest that egg should not be given to babies until twelve months of age. This egg is cooked through, but it is up to you, perhaps you could try this recipe closer to twelve months if you are more comfortable.

½ avocado

1 boiled egg, shelled

125g / 4oz can creamed corn

¼ cup / 45g / 1.5oz cous cous

Cover cous cous with water in a bowl and microwave for thirty seconds then rest for one minute. Combine avocado, egg and creamed corn to a thick paste, and combine with cous cous.

6 serves

Eggplant (aubergine), sweet potato and cous cous

½ medium size eggplant (aubergine)

½ small sweet potato

½ cup / 90g / 3oz cous cous

½ cup / 125ml / 4fl oz salt reduced beef stock (or water)

½ cup water

Cut eggplant and sweet potato into small pieces, and cook in frypan, adding water and stock until soft. Partially or fully puree to your liking. Cover cous cous with water and microwave for thirty seconds, then cover and rest for one minute. Combine with puree and serve.

6 serves

healthy baby
twelve to eighteen months

healthy baby
twelve to eighteen months

Once your baby turns one year old, he or she will start to expect more variety, texture and flavour. The following recipes include more flavour in the way of stock, tomato paste, herbs and a small amount of salt. Pureeing may not be required at all, you will be able to judge this yourself and puree if appropriate.

Start cooking from the finger foods section in addition to this section now, and give your baby a spoon or fork to hold. Help them put food onto the spoon or fork and guide to their mouth and they will soon see the fun side of using utensils. Don't expect them to be able to feed themselves yet, but keep them interested in cutlery.

These recipes make several portions, and similar to the last section, most are suitable for freezing, or will last for four days in the fridge. You should not need to cook everyday, rather keep a small selection in the fridge, and large selection in the freezer. An easy rule of thumb is to freeze half of each dish, to be used on busy week nights or when life is hectic.

Second pasta bolognese

(Follows first bolognese in previous section)

Your baby may refuse the first bolognese from the previous section by now, as they may be in search of more flavour.
Use short angel hair pasta (as shown) or serve as finger food with penne, spiralli or shell shapes.

200g / 7oz beef mince (ground meat)
1 large carrot, grated
½ small onion, diced
Handful parsley, finely chopped
3 cups / 450g / 14oz cooked pasta
200g / 7oz canned diced tomatoes
Sprinkle mixed italian herbs
2 tablespoons / 40g salt reduced tomato paste
Handful of grated cheese

Cook mince and onion in frypan, adding water to avoid sticking.
Add carrot, tomato paste and tomatoes, and simmer for half an hour, or until carrots are soft. Stir pasta into sauce with cheese.

6 serves

Scrambled eggs with ricotta and parsley

Scrambled eggs are healthy and popular with children, and are convenient and quick to make.

2 eggs

Dash of milk

Small handful parsley, finely chopped

1 tablespoon / 20g ricotta

Combine all ingredients and whisk until combined.

Cook in frypan over low heat, folding occasionally until cooked.

2 serves

Ham, vegetables and rice

*This dish is great for using up leftover rice.
To cook the rice, combine half of a cup of uncooked rice with one cup of water,
and cook in the microwave to give you one cup of cooked rice.*

½ cup / 125g / 4oz finely chopped pumpkin
½ cup / 125g / 4oz finely chopped zucchini (courgette)
2 slices lean ham, diced
1 cup / 250g / 8oz cooked rice
125g / 4oz can corn kernels
125g / 4oz can creamed corn
200g / 7oz tomato pasta sauce

Cook ham, pumpkin, corn kernels and zucchini in frypan,
adding water to avoid sticking.
Add cooked rice, creamed corn and pasta sauce and warm through.

6 serves

Gnocchi with broccoli and chicken

The mixture for this recipe is the same as that for the chicken and broccoli pies. Consider making both recipes to save on ingredients.

½ broccoli head, finely chopped

200g / 7oz chicken mince (ground meat)

2 tablespoons / 40ml cream

250g / 8oz dry gnocchi

200g / 7oz canned diced tomato

2 tablespoons / 40g reduced salt tomato paste

Boil the gnocchi in water until all pieces float.

Drain and set aside. Finely chop broccoli and cook with chicken for five minutes.

Add tomatoes and paste and simmer for ten minutes, or until broccoli is soft.

Add the cream, then combine with gnocchi and serve.

6 serves

Gnocchi with pumpkin and corn

This recipe uses half a packet of gnocchi. Consider making gnocchi with chicken and broccoli at the same time to save on ingredients.

1 cup / 250g / 8oz cooked mashed pumpkin

250g / 8oz dry gnocchi

125g / 4oz can creamed corn

125g / 4oz can corn kernels

Handful grated cheese

Boil gnocchi in water until all pieces float.

Combine remaining ingredients over heat and stir until combined.

Stir through gnocchi and serve.

6 Serves

Vegetable lasagne

This recipe is very simple. Even if you haven't made lasagne before, give it a go, you will be pleasantly surprised.

2 cups / 500g / 16oz cooked and mashed pumpkin and carrot

400g / 14oz can creamed corn

1 packet fresh or dry lasagne sheets

2 tablespoons / 45g / 1.5oz plain (all purpose) flour

2 handfulls grated cheese

1 cup / 250ml / 8fl oz milk

Combine carrot and pumpkin with creamed corn.

Place flour in small amount of the milk and stir until lumps disappear.

Add remaining milk and pour into small saucepan with grated cheese, stirring until thick.

Place small layer of vegetable mix into small greased baking tray, then place a layer of lasagne sheets on top.

Place another layer of vegetable mix onto sheet, then lay more sheets on top.

Pour a generous layer of the cheese sauce on next, then lay more sheets on top.

Continue this process until you run out of ingredients, ensuring that you finish the lasagne with cheese sauce on top.

Bake at 180°C (350°F) for thirty minutes, or until a skewer glides through the layers and the lasagne is golden brown on top.

10 Serves

Egg with bread crumbs

1 egg

1 thick slice fresh bread

Chives

Dash vinegar

Water

DIETITIAN'S TIP

Eggs are a powerhouse of nutrition, they provide complete protein, vitamins, minerals and anti-oxidants. They are a most versatile ingredient used in sweet and savoury dishes and are ideal as the basis of a quick meal such as fritatta.

Place enough water in shallow frypan to just cover an egg,

add vinegar, and set on low heat.

Crack the egg into the water (use an egg ring if you have one)

and leave for a couple of minutes,

or until the yolk is partially cooked.

Remove from water with an egg slide and place on to a plate

with chopped chives and bread crumbs on top, and mix before serving.

1 Serve

Ham and vegetable frittata

1 small carrot, grated

½ small zucchini (courgette), grated

6 free range eggs

2 slices ham, diced

125g / 4oz can corn kernels, strained

2 tablespoons / 40ml milk

Handful grated cheese

Remove excess moisture from grated vegetables by squeezing between your hands.

Combine eggs, milk and cheese in bowl and whisk with a fork.

Add corn, carrots and zucchini to egg mixture to combine, and pour into a small baking tray.

Bake for ten to fifteen minutes at 160°C (320°F)

and remove from oven as mixture is just setting on the top.

8 Serves

Apricot chicken rice

This recipe is great for using leftover rice,

or if you need to cook the rice, one cup of rice cooked in a microwave

with two cups of water will give you two cups of cooked rice.

200g / 7oz canned apricots (in natural juice), chopped

Apricot juice (from can above)

300g / 10.5oz chicken mince (ground meat)

2 cups / 500g / 16oz cooked rice

Cook chicken mince in frypan with apricot juice.

Stir through cooked rice and apricots until combined.

6 Serves

Boston (baked) beans

2 slices ham or bacon, finely chopped

400g / 14oz can kidney beans

200g / 7oz canned diced tomatoes

2 tablespoons / 40g salt reduced tomato paste

2 tablespoons / 40g honey

1 tablespoon / 20ml worcestershire sauce

Combine all ingredients and simmer for fifteen minutes until reduced.

4 serves

Pasta with vegetable sauce

If you have any leftover frozen vegetable purees in your freezer, this is a great way to use them up, substituted for the two cups below. This is a healthy recipe that is surprisingly popular.

2 cups / 350g / 12oz chopped vegetables

eg. carrot, pumpkin, zucchini (courgette), sweet potato, peas

3 cups / 450g / 16oz cooked pasta

Sprinkle mixed dried herbs

Handful grated cheese

Steam the vegetables and puree. Add to small saucepan and simmer with herbs for two minutes. Add pasta and cheese to combine. Serve.

6 serves

Ham and vegetable ratatouille

This dish can be served with brown rice, pasta, cous cous or on its own.

½ small eggplant (aubergine), chopped
½ small red capsicum (bell pepper), chopped
½ small zucchini (courgette) chopped
3 slices lean ham, chopped
400g / 14oz canned diced tomatoes
1 tablespoon / 40g salt reduced tomato paste
Sprinkle mixed herbs
Handful parsley, chopped

Simmer vegetables with herbs, tomatoes and tomato paste for fifteen minutes, or until vegetables are soft.
Add ham and chopped parsley and serve.

6 Serves

Brown lentils with ham

½ red capsicum (bell pepper), diced

½ green capsicum (bell pepper), diced

¼ brown onion, diced

3 slices lean ham, diced

400g / 14oz can of brown lentils, drained

2 tablespoons / 40g salt reduced tomato paste

Handful grated cheese

Cook ham, onion and capsicum in fry pan, adding water to avoid sticking. After five minutes, add tomato paste and drained lentils and stir to cook for two minutes. Stir cheese through and serve.

4 Serves

Sausages and pasta

Preservative free sausages can be purchased from your local butcher.

4 lean preservative free sausages

2 cups / 300g / 10.5oz cooked pasta

1 cup / 250ml / 8fl oz tomato pasta sauce

Sprinkle mixed herbs

Chop sausages into bite size pieces and cook in frypan.

Drain any fat, then add pasta sauce and herbs and stir

on low heat for two minutes. Add cooked pasta and stir through.

4 Serves

Cheesy maccaroni

300g / 10.5oz dry maccaroni
3 tablespoons / 60g butter
2 tablespoons / 40g flour

1 ½ cups / 375ml / 12fl oz milk
1 ½ cups / 375g / 12oz grated cheese

DIETITIAN'S TIP

Pasta is a food most kids love, luckily it is very good for them too. Pasta is rich in carbohydrate, protein and B vitamins. The carbohydrate is more slowly digested than that provided by potato and some rices so it gives longer lasting energy.

Boil the maccaroni until soft, drain and set aside.

Melt butter in fry pan, and add flour, mixing to a paste.

Slowly add milk to frypan, using a whisk to remove lumps. Simmer for five minutes, turn the heat off, add cheese and stir until melted. Combine maccaroni and sauce in fry pan, and stir over low heat until all cheese is melted and combined with pasta.

6 Serves

healthy baby

eighteen to twenty four months

healthy baby
eighteen to twenty four months

Your baby will have tasted and enjoyed a variety of flavours by this stage, and the following section provides more recipes with added texture, flavour and variety. You may experience a fussy eater during this stage and if so, don't despair, there are some suggestions later in this book that you may wish to refer to.

Almost every recipe following is suitable for the whole family, as your baby will be eating a lot of the same foods as you are now.

Continue using the finger foods section of the book, and challenging your baby with the excitement of a fork or spoon. Offer a variety of spoon fed and finger food to keep meals interesting.

Chicken and mushroom quiche

Try replacing the chicken and mushroom with alternate fillings such as tomato and ham, spinach and cheese, grated carrot and zucchini or tuna and peas.

200g / 7oz chicken mince (ground meat)
6 button mushrooms, diced
½ small onion, diced
2 handfuls grated cheese
5 eggs
½ cup / 125ml milk
Handful chopped chives
1 sheet shortcrust pastry

Lay pastry over a pie flan, or any baking dish that fits the pastry, and cut extra pastry from overhanging edges. Ensure all sides are intact, and fill in any holes with off cuts of pastry. Prick base with a fork and bake the empty crust for 10 minutes at 170°C (340°F), then remove from oven to rest. Cook chicken, mushrooms and onion in fry pan for five minutes or until cooked. Lightly beat eggs, add filling and remaining ingredients. Add mixture to crust and bake for 15 minutes at 170°C (340°F), or until egg mix is just set. Slice and serve.

8 Serves

Shepherds pie

The first part of this recipe makes a sheperds pie or spaghetti bolognese sauce. Consider doubling the recipe and using half for a sheperds pie, and the other half for a bolognese.

400g / 14oz beef mince (ground meat)
2 carrots, grated
1 onion, diced
Sprinkle mixed italian herbs
3 tablespoons / 60g reduced salt tomato paste

Handful parsley, finely chopped
2 large potatoes, chopped
400g / 14oz canned diced tomatoes
Dash of milk
Handful grated cheese

Cook mince with onion in frypan, adding water to avoid sticking. Add carrot, peas, tomato paste and tomatoes, and simmer for half an hour, or until carrots are soft. Pour into a baking tray or roasting pan. Boil chopped potatoes, add milk and cheese and mash to a thick consistency. Pour on top of the sauce, and sprinkle cheese on top.

Bake at 170°C (340°F) for fifteen to twenty minutes, or until light brown on top.

8 Serves

Fried rice with egg

This recipe is great for using leftover or pre cooked rice. If you need to cook it, a cup of rice cooked in a microwave with two cups of water will give you two cups of cooked rice.

- 3 slices ham or bacon, diced
- 2 cups / 500g / 16oz cooked rice
- 125g / 4oz can corn kernels
- ½ carrot, diced
- 1 egg
- 2 handfuls frozen peas
- 2 tablespoons / 40ml soy sauce

Add ham to pan, with rice, corn, peas and soy sauce, stirring for two minutes. Whisk egg in a bowl and stir through at the last minute, until cooked.

6 Serves

Chicken and pea risotto

1 chicken breast, diced
or 200g / 7oz chicken mince (ground meat)
½ small onion, diced
Handful parsley, chopped
Handful grated cheese

1 cup / 175g / 6oz frozen (or fresh) peas
1 cup / 190g / 7oz Arborio rice
1 cup / 250ml reduced salt chicken stock
1 cup / 250ml water
Dash of olive oil

Cook chicken with onion in a frypan, adding a small amount of olive oil to avoid sticking. Add washed rice and stir to coat rice. Add half a cup of stock and stir on medium heat until rice absorbs stock. Add another half cup of stock, lower heat and stir until absorbed, then add cup of water, and simmer on low, stirring occasionally. Add more water if the risotto is looking dry, and keep simmering until rice is cooked (test by biting a rice grain). Add peas and leave for a couple of minutes until cooked through. Add cheese and stir through.

8 Serves

Scrambled tomato eggs

2 eggs

2 tablespoons milk

Handful grated cheese

1 teaspoon / 5g tomato paste

Handful parsley, chopped

1 slice of toast

Whisk eggs, tomato paste and milk and cook in a fry pan on low for several minutes, folding over mixture until cooked. Add cheese, parsley and serve.

2 Serves

Pasta with pork

Choose pasta shapes that can be held by little fingers such as penne, spiral or shell.

200g / 7oz pork loin
¼ small brown onion, diced
½ small zucchini
(courgette) finely grated
200g / 7oz canned diced tomatoes
1 tablespoon / 20g reduced salt
tomato paste
Handful grated cheese
Sprinkle mixed herbs
2 cups / 300g / 10.5oz cooked pasta

Cook tomato, mixed herbs, tomato paste and onion in frypan for five minutes. Add pork and stir on medium heat until pork is cooked through. Stir through zucchini and cooked pasta for a couple of minutes, then add grated cheese and stir through.

8 serves

Roast pork with gravy

You may wish to make this recipe for the whole family, using a large loin of pork, and a variety of different vegetables.

100g / 3.5oz pork loin
¼ carrot, cut into bite size pieces
½ potato, cut into bite size pieces
Handful frozen peas
Sprinkle mixed herbs
Salt reduced pre-prepared gravy

Place carrot and potato on baking tray, and lay pork loin in amongst the vegetables. Add herbs and a small amount of olive oil. Bake in oven at 180°C (355°F) for twenty minutes, or until vegetables and pork are cooked. Cook peas in a bowl in the microwave for thirty seconds, or until cooked. Slice pork into bite size pieces and combine with all vegetables in a serving bowl. Heat up gravy as per packet instructions and pour a small amount over pork and vegetables.

2 serves

Lasagne

400g / 14oz beef mince (ground meat)
2 carrots, grated
1 small onion, diced
Large handful parsley, chopped
Sprinkle mixed italian herbs
3 tablespoons / 60g
   reduced salt tomato paste
400g / 14oz canned diced tomatoes
1 packet fresh or dry lasagne sheets
2 handfuls grated cheese
1 cup / 250ml / 8fl oz milk
3 tablespoons / 45g / 1.5oz
   plain (all purpose) flour

Brown mince and onion in fry pan for five minutes, then add tomato paste, tomatoes, herbs and carrot, and simmer for half an hour on low heat. Mix flour in a small amount of the milk, to make a thin paste. Add remaining milk and pour into small saucepan with grated cheese, stirring until thick. Place small layer of meat mixture into small baking tray, then place one layer of lasagne sheets on top. Place another layer of meat onto sheet, and then lay more sheets on top. Pour a generous layer of the cheese sauce on next, then lay more sheets on top. Continue this process until you run out of ingredients, ensuring that you finish the lasagne with cheese sauce on top. Bake at 180°C (355°F) for thirty minutes, or until a skewer glides through the layers and the lasagne is golden brown on top.

10 serves

Chicken and vegetable soup

Once pureed, this healthy soup should be thick, so that your baby can eat it with their favourite spoon. Yes, there will be a mess, but your baby will have so much fun learning how to use a spoon.

½ carrot, diced

½ zucchini (courgette), diced

Handful of peas

100g / 3.5oz chicken mince (ground meat) OR leftover piece of chicken chopped

½ cup / 70g / 2.5oz red lentils

2 cups / 500ml /16fl oz reduced salt chicken stock

Sprinkle mixed herbs

125g / 4oz can corn kernels

Handful grated cheese

Combine all ingredients into saucepan and simmer on low heat for half an hour, or until carrots are soft. Puree to a thick consistency.

6 serves

Sweet and sour pork

This recipe can be served with rice, or on its own.

1cm size pieces

100g / 3.5oz pork loin or leftover roast pork

½ small red capsicum (bell pepper)

½ carrot

¼ broccoli head

¼ cup / 50g canned diced pineapple

For the sauce

2 tablespoons / 40ml pineapple juice, leftover from the can

1 tablespoon / 20ml soy sauce

Dash of honey

1 tablespoon / 20g plain flour

2 tablespoons / 40ml water

Start cooking carrot in frypan, adding water to avoid sticking,
and after three minutes, add the pork, broccoli and capsicum.
Combine sauce ingredients in small bowl or cup, stirring to combine.
When pork is cooked and vegetables are semi-soft, pour sauce over and heat through.

3 serves

Fish and vegetables

All ingredients to be cut into bite size pieces:

Small piece white flesh fish such as flake / sole / hake / cod / snapper

½ red capsicum (bell pepper)

½ small zucchini (courgette)

¼ broccoli head

Small piece sweet potato

Sprinkle season-all*

Sprinkle mixed herbs

Olive oil

* Season-All is a dry mix of several ground herbs, and contains some salt

DIETITIAN'S TIP

Not only does broccoli contain anti-oxidants including Vitamin C but it is an excellent source of folate. Broccoli also contains a phytochemical that has specific anti-cancer properties. Call it "little trees" and children love it.

Add a dash of olive oil to a frypan, then toss sweet potato around for five minutes on medium heat, adding water to avoid sticking. Add capsicum (bell pepper), zucchini (courgette) and broccoli, and toss for a further five to ten minutes, or until all vegetables are cooked. Add fish, season-all and herbs and toss very gently until fish is cooked through.

4 serves

Ham and zucchini (courgette) soup

*Once pureed, this healthy soup should be thick,
so that your baby can eat it with their favourite spoon.
Yes, there will be a mess, but your baby will have so much fun learning how to use a spoon.*

1 small zucchini (courgette), diced

1 medium size potato, diced

¼ onion, diced

3 slices ham, diced

500ml / 2 cups / 16fl oz salt reduced chicken stock

Tablespoon / 20ml cream

Place all ingredients except for the cream into a saucepan and simmer
on low heat for thirty minutes, or until potato is cooked through.
Puree to a thick consistency, add cream and stir through.

4 serves

Tuna pasta bake

3 cups / 450g / 15oz cooked pasta
¼ onion diced
400g / 14oz can tuna
400g / 14oz can creamed corn

125g / 4oz can corn kernels
½ cup / 125ml / 4fl oz cream
2 handfuls grated cheese
Extra cheese

Cook onion in fry pan for two minutes, then add remaining ingredients, except the pasta, and stir to a thick sauce. Stir through the pasta then pour mixture into a baking dish and sprinkle extra cheese on top. Bake at 170°C (340°F) for twenty minutes, or until brown on top. Slice into portions.

8 serves

Chicken and vegetable cous cous

This recipe is great for warm weather as it can be served cold. If you want to roast the capsicum yourself, simply place whole red capsicum in the oven at 200°C (390°F) for ten to twenty minutes, or until skin starts to blister. Then place in a plastic bag to sweat for five minutes, remove skin and slice.

2 handfulls chopped roasted red capsicum (bell pepper)
Handful chopped parsley
1 chicken breast
½ cup / 125g / 4oz frozen peas, defrosted
125g / 4oz can corn kernels, drained
½ cup / 90g / 3oz dry cous cous
1 cup / 250ml / 8fl oz chicken stock
Olive oil
2 tablespoons / 40ml white vinegar
Pinch of salt

Pour a dash of olive oil over chicken breast, and grill on stove top or under griller for ten minutes, or until cooked through. If chicken breast is thick, slice into three pieces to shorten grilling time. Slice chicken into small pieces. Combine cous cous with stock in a small saucepan and simmer on low heat for five minutes, then rest and cover for five minutes. Combine all ingredients in a large bowl, and toss to combine.

4 serves

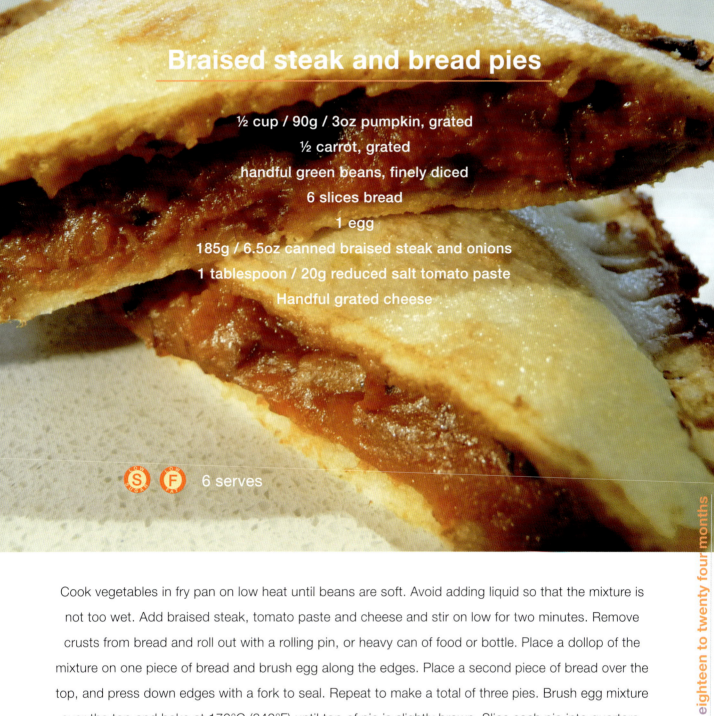

Braised steak and bread pies

½ cup / 90g / 3oz pumpkin, grated
½ carrot, grated
handful green beans, finely diced
6 slices bread
1 egg
185g / 6.5oz canned braised steak and onions
1 tablespoon / 20g reduced salt tomato paste
Handful grated cheese

6 serves

Cook vegetables in fry pan on low heat until beans are soft. Avoid adding liquid so that the mixture is not too wet. Add braised steak, tomato paste and cheese and stir on low for two minutes. Remove crusts from bread and roll out with a rolling pin, or heavy can of food or bottle. Place a dollop of the mixture on one piece of bread and brush egg along the edges. Place a second piece of bread over the top, and press down edges with a fork to seal. Repeat to make a total of three pies. Brush egg mixture over the top and bake at 170°C (340°F) until top of pie is slightly brown. Slice each pie into quarters.

Meatballs

This recipe is delicious served with cooked pasta, cous cous or rice.

400g / 14oz beef mince (ground meat)
2 tablespoons / 40g salt reduced tomato paste
Sprinkle mixed dried herbs
1 egg

½ cup / 30g / 1oz breadcrumbs
Handful chopped parsley
Olive oil
½ cup / 125ml / 4oz tomato pasta sauce

DIETITIAN'S TIP

Lean red meat is the best source of readily available iron, which is essential for brain development. Lean red meat is also rch in zinc which boosts immune function. Make sure to choose lean cuts or the leanest mince (ground meat) to minimise saturated fat.

Mix all ingredients except olive oil and tomato sauce and shape into small balls. Fry in the smallest amount of olive oil until lightly brown on all sides and coat in tomato sauce.

4 Serves

Chicken pasta bake

½ cup / 125g / 4oz roasted red capsicum (bell pepper)
1 chicken breast, diced
2 bacon rashers, diced
¼ onion, diced
2 handfulls frozen peas

3 cups / 450g / 15oz cooked pasta
2 tablespoons / 40g reduced salt tomato paste
½ cup / 125ml / 4fl oz cream
2 handfulls grated cheese
Extra cheese

Brown chicken, onion and bacon in fry pan, and drain excess oil. Add remaining ingredients to combine, adding pasta last. Pour into baking dish and sprinkle extra cheese on top. Bake at 170°C (340°F) for twenty minutes, or until brown on top. Slice into portions.

8 serves

Potato and leek soup

Once pureed, this healthy soup should be thick, so that your baby can eat it with their favourite spoon. Yes, there will be a mess, but your baby will have so much fun learning how to use a spoon.

3 medium size potatoes, peeled and cut into pieces
1 leek, outer layer removed and chopped into discs
¼ onion, diced
2 chicken stock cubes
3 slices of ham or bacon, diced
2 cups / 500ml / 16fl oz water

Cook onion and ham or bacon in fry pan until soft. Combine all ingredients into a saucepan and simmer on low heat for thirty minutes, or until potato is soft. You may need to add more water, depending on the size of the potatoes. Puree and serve with a spoon.

8 serves

Chicken and bacon slow cook

5 chicken thighs

5 lean bacon rashers

5 baby potatoes, cut in half

½ red capsicum (bell pepper), cut to 2cm pieces

½ zucchini (courgette), cut to 2cm pieces

2 cups / 500ml / 16fl oz tomato pasta sauce

Sprinkle mixed dried herbs

1 cup / 180g / 6oz cous cous

Handful grated cheese

Toothpicks

Wrap each chicken thigh in a bacon rasher, and secure with two toothpicks. Place in bottom of slow cooker, and add tomato puree and mixed herbs, then set on low heat. After one hour, add the potatoes, and after another hour, add the zucchini and capsicum. After another hour, or a total of three hours, check to see that the potatoes are cooked through, then turn off the heat. Cook cous cous in a small saucepan in two cups of water on medium heat for three minutes, then put a lid on the pan and rest for two minutes, or until cous cous is soft. Slice half a chicken thigh with vegetables on a small amount of the cous cous and sprinkle grated cheese on the top.

10 serves

Chicken noodles with vegetables

150g / 5oz dry rice noodles

200g / 7oz chicken mince (ground meat)

1 grated carrot

½ diced capsicum (bell pepper)

50g / 1.8oz frozen spinach

¼ cauliflower, cut into tiny florets

2 tablespoons / 40ml soy sauce

Dash honey

Water

Soak noodles in boiling hot water for half an hour, or until soft and ready to use. Cook chicken, capsicum and cauliflower in frypan for five minutes, adding water to avoid sticking. Add soy sauce and honey, and remaining ingredients and cook for a further five minutes.

6 serves

Beef stroganoff

300g / 10.5oz beef strips

¼ diced onion

½ red capsicum (bell pepper), cut into 2cm pieces

½ cup / 125ml / 4fl oz cream

½ cup / 125ml / 4fl oz milk

2 tablespooons / 40g reduced salt tomato paste

2 tablespoons / 40ml worcestershire sauce

Brown onion, capsicum and beef in frypan, adding water to avoid sticking. Mix remaining ingredients in a bowl to combine and pour over meat and vegetables. Simmer for a further five minutes, or until meat and vegetables are cooked through. Serve with rice, pasta or cous cous.

8 Serves

Mexican wraps

You may have leftover mixture from this recipe, which can be spread on toast for a yummy meal.

½ zucchini (courgette), grated
½ carrot, grated
5 tortilla wraps
125g / 4oz can corn kernels
125g / 4oz can red kidney beans

200g / 7fl oz jar mild taco sauce
1 cup / 250g / 8oz cooked brown rice
(can use pre-cooked from supermarket)
200g / 7oz can refried beans
Handfulls grated cheese

Combine zucchini, carrot, corn, beans, refried beans, rice, half of the jar taco sauce and half of the cheese in a bowl and mix to combine. Lay a wrap flat, and dollop the mixture in a central strip from one end to the other. Roll the wrap so that the strip of mixture is surrounded. Place in a baking tray, and repeat with the remaining wraps. Pour the remaining taco sauce over the wraps and sprinkle with the remaining cheese. Bake at 170°C (340°F) for twenty minutes, or until the top has browned. Slice wraps into bite size pieces to serve.

8 Serves

healthy baby finger foods

healthy baby finger foods

Every baby is different, and at some stage your baby will start to enjoy picking up foods and placing them in their mouth. Babies who cut teeth earlier than most may be interested in finger foods earlier, as they are able to chew, but babies with no teeth still enjoy the texture of finger foods, and can soften the food before swallowing.

Make sure your baby can sit upright before starting solids and don't give finger foods (or any solids) to babies laying down (choking hazard).

The first finger foods offered should be soft and easily broken up, so as to avoid the risk of choking. Steamed vegetables such as carrot, green beans, broccoli, pumpkin, sweet potato and red capsicum are good ideas, and small pieces of cracker biscuit or toast are also popular.

At around nine months old you may wish to start offering some finger foods, or earlier if you think your baby is ready.

Once your baby has tolerated the simple ideas just mentioned, it is time to create some delicious hand held foods for your baby.

In the fussy eaters section following, I mention the independence factor, and this is where babies sometimes refuse to eat from a spoon that you hold, purely because they want to hold their food themselves. This section provides many ideas for keeping harmony when this happens.

Sandwich ideas

Toddlers love sandwiches, and this recipe is a list of ideas for quick and easy sandwich fillings, great for lunches. Some babies will remove the filling and eat the bread only, and some will remove the filling and eat this part only, so consider putting ingredients in a small blender, or mashing with a fork to make the filling stick to the bread.

Ham and cheese
Avocado
Chicken and Avocado
Tuna and cheese
Tuna and avocado
Tuna and creamed corn
Mashed banana
Egg and mayonaise
Corned beef
Cream cheese
Cheese spread
Honey
Jam
Cheese and vegemite

Dips such as:
hummus,
red capsicum,
tzatziki
or babbaganoush

DIETITIAN'S TIP

Multi-grain bread has more healthy fats and fibre than white bead does. The grains and fat slow down the release of glucose, helping energy last longer.

Spinach and cheese pie

½ small onion, diced

150g / 5oz frozen / fresh spinach

100g / 3.5oz ricotta

2 handfuls grated cheese

10 sheets filo pastry (dough)

Pinch salt

1 egg

2 tablespoons / 40ml milk

DIETITIAN'S TIP

Filo pastry is a great alternative o higher fat pastries, it can be used in place of puff and short crust pastry. Brush between the sheets with milk or juice instead of oil to keep the fat content low.

Cook spinach or thaw if frozen, drain excess moisture and mix with remaining ingredients, except for pastry. Take filo pastry and cut sheets in half. Find a baking tray that will fit the sheets, with a slight overlap. Spread milk across each half pastry sheet, layering ten into the baking tray. Add spinach mixture and top with ten additional half filo sheets, brushed with milk. Ensure that the top of the pie is brushed with butter. Tuck pastry edges down the side of the baking tray and place in oven. Bake at 170°C (340°F) for fifteen minutes, or until brown on the top.

6 serves

Pasta cakes

The concept of this recipe can be applied to any leftover pasta, and provides a great solution if your baby refuses food from a fork or spoon held by you. Simply add an egg to your leftover pasta and bake as cakes.

½ carrot, grated

¼ onion, diced

2 tablespoons / 40g fresh or canned tomato diced

200g / 7oz beef mince (ground meat)

2 cups / 300g / 10oz cooked pasta

2 tablespoons / 40g reduced salt tomato paste

1 tablespoon / 20ml cream

Large handful grated cheese

1 egg, whisked

Brown mince and onion, then add carrot, tomato paste and tomato.
Simmer for ten minutes, then allow to cool. Add egg and pasta and stir to combine.
Place mixture into mini muffin tin and bake for
ten to twelve minutes at 170°C (340°F) or until set.
Allow to cool, then run a knife around edge of muffin hole and slide out.

10 serves

Lamb skewers

These skewers are delicious served with tzatziki greek dip, and are great eaten warm or cold.

200g / 7oz tender lamb pieces

¼ red capsicum (bell pepper), cut into 2cm pieces

¼ green capsicum (bell pepper), cut into 2cm pieces

½ cup / 125g / 4oz fresh or canned pineapple pieces

Dash of olive oil

Skewers

Place ingredients onto skewers and drizzle olive oil over the top.

Grill for five to ten minutes until cooked. Remove from skewers and serve.

4 serves

Chicken and vegetable scrolls

½ cup / 125g / 4oz pumpkin, grated
200g / 7oz chicken mince (ground meat)
½ cup / 125g / 4oz spinach frozen or fresh, wilted
1 sheet puff pastry
2 tablespoons / 40g reduced salt tomato paste
Sprinkle mixed herbs
Olive oil spray
Large handful grated cheese

Remove pastry from pack, leaving plastic film on one side. Spread tomato paste onto the exposed side of the pastry. Combine chicken mince, cheese, pumpkin, spinach and mixed herbs. Spread mixture onto pastry, spreading evenly across whole sheet. Roll from one end to the other slowly, forming a coil, until one side meets the other end of the pastry. Slice into discs, and place on baking tray sprayed with olive oil spray. Bake for twenty five minutes at 170°C (340°F), or until brown.

Makes 12

Roast lamb patties

This recipe is best made with leftover roast lamb and vegetables, otherwise you will need to roast a piece of lamb with vegetables for twenty minutes at 180°C (350°F), allow to cool, then make the recipe. This recipe could be used with any leftover roast meat and vegetables.

2 cups / 300g / 10oz finely chopped roasted lamb and vegetables
2 eggs, whisked
½ cup / 60g / 2oz plain (all purpose) flour
2 tablespoons / 40ml milk
Handful cheese
Pinch salt
Olive oil

Combine all ingredients and mix until thick, adding more flour or milk if too runny or thick. Cook in a small amount of olive oil, adding spoonfuls of mixture and cook on both sides. Serve alone or with natural yoghurt.

Makes 10

Spring rolls

Large spring roll wrappers

200g / 7oz chicken mince (ground meat)

½ carrot, grated

Handful frozen peas

125g / 4oz canned corn kernels, drained

3 tablespoons / 60ml soy sauce

Dash of honey

Small handful chopped coriander

1 egg

Olive oil spray

Dice onion and cook with chicken mince for five minutes in frypan, adding a small amount of water to avoid sticking. Grate carrot and add to mince. Add remaining ingredients and stir to combine, ensuring that mixture does not contain too much water. Lay a wrapper on bench surface, at a angle to form a diamond shape and lay a line of mixture just below the centre, horizontally. Fold smaller end over the mixture, fold in sides, then roll until cylinder shape is achieved. Whisk egg, and add a tiny amount to join edges of pastry to hold. Spray with a small amount of olive oil and bake on baking tray at 170°C (340°F) for ten minutes, or shallow fry in olive oil.

Makes 10

Pasty Slice

Some of you may assume pasty slice to be difficult to make, and I hope this recipe will pleasantly surprise you. This recipe stretches a long way and is healthy and delicious. Use a food processor (bowl with rotating blade) to finely dice each ingredient for a faster preparation time. Freezes well.

Finely diced

1 cup / 175g / 6oz onion
3 cups / 500g / 16oz pumpkin
3 cups / 500g / 16oz potato
2 cups / 350g / 12oz carrot

500g / 16oz beef mince (ground meat)
Sprinkle ground white pepper
1 tablespoon / 15g / .5oz season all *
4 tablespoons / 60g / 2oz plain (all purpose) flour
4 sheets shortcrust pastry

* Season-all is a dry mix of several ground herbs, and contains some salt

Combine all ingredients, except for pastry in a large bowl, using clean hands to mix. Divide mixture into four, and pile onto each sheet of pastry, so that you form a long, wide log shape when wrapped. Close sides along the length of the mixture and press pastry to meet and close. Turn over and press ends together to close each slice. Bake at 170°C (340°F) for twenty minutes, or until brown on the top. Once cooked, slice to serve.

Makes 30 serves

Toddler Pizza

Optional: To avoid your baby picking the topping off, it is a good idea to put the topping ingredients in a blender to form a paste.

½ red capsicum (bell pepper), finely diced
½ green capsicum (bell pepper), finely diced
Handful button mushrooms, finely diced
1 pack wholemeal English muffins
3 tablespons / 60g salt reduced tomato paste
Handful grated cheese

Cut muffins in half and spread tomato paste onto each one. Combine capsicum and mushrooms and spread onto each muffin, then sprinkle grated cheese on top. Cook for ten minutes at 180°C (355°F)

Optional extras –

chopped lean ham, pineapple, left over chicken, tomato, pumpkin

Serves 10

Flat bread toasties

This recipe ideally requires a sandwich press/grill.
If you don't have one, you can try using the grill of your oven.
Flat bread can be found in the bread section of the supermarket, they are circular and flat.

1 tomato, sliced
3 slices of ham
2 pieces of flatbread
Handful grated cheese

Alternate fillings:

1. Baby spinach, canned tuna, tomato and cheese
2. Corned beef and tomato
3. Cooked mushrooms, ham and cheese
4. Chicken and mayonaise

Cut edge of flat bread and carefully separate sides to form a pocket.
Place sliced ham, tomato and grated cheese inside and close.
Place inside griller and cook for five minutes or until slightly brown.
Slice into triangles

Makes 16 triangles

Chicken and vegetable sausage rolls

1 carrot, grated and squeezed to remove excess moisture

½ red capsicum (bell pepper), diced

1 small onion, diced

2 handfulls frozen peas

300g / 10.5oz chicken mince (ground meat)

Sprinkle mixed herbs

2 sheets puff pastry

2 tablespoons / 40g reduced salt tomato paste

DIETITIAN'S TIP

Corn is delicious on its own or in a meal, it is a good source of vitamins and fibre and slowly digested carbohydrate.

Corn is a favourite with kids due to its naturally sweet flavour.

Combine all ingredients except for the pastry. Cut pastry sheets in half and place a line of the mixture down the middle of each half pastry sheet, adding enough so that, by rolling the pastry around the mixture, the sheet will slightly overlap. Wrap the mixture, and press on the overlapping pastry to close the roll. Cut into bite size pieces and bake on baking tray at 180°C (350°F) for ten to fifteen minutes, or until pastry is brown and rolls are cooked through.

Makes 24

Ham and vegetable slice

1 zucchini (courgette), grated and squeezed to remove excess moisture

½ carrot, grated and squeezed to remove excess moisture

1 onion, finely diced

1 cup / 175g / 6oz frozen pea and corn mix

3 slices ham, finely diced

1 cup / 125g / 4oz self raising flour

½ cup / 125g / 4fl oz olive oil

5 eggs

3 handfulls grated cheese

Combine all ingredients and pour into greased or lined baking tin and cook at 170°C (340°F) until brown on the top.

Cut into hand held portions.

Makes 20 portions

Pumpkin and cheese balls

1 cup / 175g / 6oz pumpkin, grated
125g / 4oz canned corn kernels, drained
Handful chopped parsley
1 cup / 250g / 8oz cooked rice
2 tablespoons / 30g / 1oz plain (all purpose) flour
½ cup / 60g / 2oz breadcrumbs
2 eggs
Large handful grated cheese

Combine pumpkin, corn, parsley, cheese, rice, flour and one egg in large bowl.
The mixture is the right consistency if it doesn't stick to your hand when you pick up a handful.
If it is too wet, add some more flour, if it is too dry, add some water.
Roll mixture into balls, coat in breadcrumbs, dip in beaten egg, then back into breadcrumbs.
Place on baking tray sprayed with olive oil, and spray balls lightly with olive oil.
Bake at 170°C (340°F) for ten to fifteen minutes, or until slightly brown.
Alternatively shallow fry in olive oil.

Makes 20 portions

Roasted vegetable medley

This recipe is tasty served with yoghurt or grated cheese.

2 cups / 350g / 12oz chopped vegetables of your choice:

Carrot, pumpkin, sweet potato, potato

Green beans, cauliflower, zucchini (courgette)

Sprinkle mixed dried herbs

Olive oil

Pinch salt

DIETITIAN'S TIP

Herbs not only add flavour to foods, they are an excellent source of anti-oxidants. The aromatic flavours and aromas are related to a vast range of natural compounds in the herbs. Research is showing benefits including reduced cancer risk, antivial properties and reduced heart disease linked to these compounds.

Place chopped vegetables in baking tray, sprinkle with dried herbs and salt and pour over a small amount of olive oil, tossing to coat. Roast in oven for twenty minutes at 170°C (340°F), or until slightly brown and cooked through.
Green vegetables and cauliflower should be added half way through the cooking process, as they don't take as long as potato, pumpkin and carrot.

2 serves

Chicken croquettes

200g / 7oz chicken mince (ground meat)

½ carrot, grated and squeezed to remove excess moisture

½ cup / 125g / 4oz mashed potato

125g / 4oz canned corn kernels

Large handful frozen peas

2 eggs

4 tablespoons / 15g / .5oz breadcrumbs

Handful grated cheese

Sprinkle mixed herbs

Pinch salt

Olive oil spray

Olive oil

Place one egg and two tabelspoons of breadcrumbs aside. Combine all remaining ingredients, to form a mixture that does not stick to your hand when you pick it up, adding more flour if required. Whisk remaining egg in small bowl and pour breadcrumbs into a second small bowl. Roll chicken mixture into cylinders and coat lightly in breadcrumbs, then in egg, then again in breadcrumbs. Ensure croquette is dry to the touch. Spray with olive oil and bake for ten minutes at 180°C (350°F), or shallow fry in olive oil until brown.

Makes 15

Tuna patties

1 cup / 250g / 8oz mashed potato

1 egg

200g / 7oz canned tuna

½ cup / 80g / 3oz frozen pea and corn mix

Sprinkle mixed herbs

1 cup / 100g / 3.5oz rolled oats

Olive oil

DIETITIAN'S TIP

Fish is a good source of omega 3 fats, the oilier the fish the higher the omega 3 fats. Eating fish regularly is very good for the brain and eyes. Children who eat fish may be less likely to develop asthma and depression.

Combine all ingredients, except for olive oil, and shape into patties. Mixture should not stick between your fingers, if it does add some more rolled oats until the mixture is mouldable. Shallow fry in minimal olive oil, until light brown on either side.

Makes 20

Beef rissoles

400g / 14oz beef mince (ground meat)

2 tablespoons / 40g reduced salt tomato paste

Sprinkle mixed dried herbs

1 egg

½ cup / 30g / 1oz breadcrumbs

Handful chopped parsley

Olive oil

Mix all ingredients and shape into patties, adding more bread crumbs if mixture is too wet. Fry in a small amount of olive oil, until lightly brown on all sides.

Makes 20

Pumpkin and bean squares

DIETITIAN'S TIP

Legumes (eg. beans) are naturally low in fat and high in fibre, they are a great source of protein in a vegetarian meal. Legumes are also rich in B vitamins and minerals. The carbohydrate is very slowly digested to keep us full fo longer.

1 cup / 250g / 8oz cooked, mashed pumpkin
125g / 4oz canned corn kernels
125g / 4oz canned mixed beans
125g / 4oz canned creamed corn
1 sheet puff pastry
Handful grated cheese
1 tablespoon / 20g reduced salt tomato paste
Olive oil spray

Combine all ingredients except for pastry. Cut pastry sheet in quarters, and pile pumpkin mixture onto the middle of each square. Bring the corners of the square in to meet, pinch together to close and spray with olive oil spray. Bake at 170°C (340°F) for ten to twelve minutes or until brown.

Makes 4 squares

Schnitzel fingers

> **DIETITIAN'S TIP**
>
> Schnitzel fingers are a great way to serve meat to fussy eaters and would be delicious as part of a main meal with salad or mashed potato and vegetables.

1 large piece tenderised round or minute steak
1 egg
2 tablespoons / 40ml milk
1 cup / 60g / 2oz breadcrumbs
Olive oil

Cut steak into finger size pieces, perhaps 3cm x 8cm. Whisk egg in a bowl, and add milk. Place breadcrumbs into a bowl. Coat steak in breadcrumbs, then dip in egg/milk mix, then recoat with breadcrumbs thoroughly. Press down to ensure breadcrumbs stick, and coat again if it looks too moist.
Add olive oil to pan on medium heat, and add fingers.
After two minutes, check underside, and when light brown, turn over for a couple of minutes. Remove from pan and drain on paper towel.

Makes 8

Toast ideas

Similar to the sandwich ideas page, the following list of ideas for toast represents different ways to keep toast interesting as an easy and quick meal. Most can be cooked under the griller. Some babies will remove the topping and eat the toast only, and some will remove the topping and eat the topping only, so consider putting ingredients in a small blender, or mashing with a fork to make the filling stick to the bread.

Dip such as hummus, red capsicum (bell pepper), tzatziki or babbaganoush

Grated cheese, worcestershire sauce and diced bacon

Mashed red kidney beans, tomato paste and cheese

Cream cheese and mashed red kidney beans

Bacon and banana (see separate recipe)

Mashed soft boiled egg

Cheese spread and vegemite

Tomato paste and cheese

Tuna and creamed corn

Cheese and vegemite

Avocado and cheese

Tuna and cheese

Ham and cheese

Mashed banana

Creamed corn

Cream cheese

Fruit toast

Honey

Jam

Ham and polenta squares

This recipe is designed to make soft squares. As your child gets older reduce the water for a firmer result.

¼ onion, diced

3 slices ham, diced

½ cup / 90g / 3oz quick cooking polenta

2 cups / 500ml / 16fl oz of water

Large handful grated cheese

Cook onion and ham in frypan, adding water to avoid sticking. Bring water to the boil in a saucepan, and slowly pour dry polenta in. Keep stirring for two minutes, until polenta starts to thicken, then add ham, onion and cheese and stir for two more minutes. Pour into small tray and let rest for twenty minutes, or until set.

Optional - grill the top until light brown.

Cut into squares and serve.

Makes 10

Pea and corn fritters

2 large handfulls frozen peas

125g / 4oz canned corn kernels, drained

100g / 3.5oz hummus dip

¼ cup / 30g / 1oz plain (all purpose) flour

1 egg

Olive oil

DIETITIAN'S TIP

Hummus is made from chick peas, tahini, olive oil, garlic and lemon juice, making it a very healthy food. Hummus is high in fibre, a good source or protein and slowly digested carbohydrate. It also has healthy fats from the sesame seeds and olive oil.

Mix ingredients except oil in bowl and cook spoonfulls in a small amount of olive oil in a frypan. Cook on both sides until brown.

Makes 10

Bacon and banana toast

This recipe is great for fussy eaters, and is quick and easy to make.

½ banana, mashed with a fork

1 rasher of bacon, finely diced

Handful grated cheese

2 pieces of bread

Toast bread to light brown. Cook bacon in small saucepan for two minutes and set aside. Spread banana onto toast, and top with bacon mixture and cheese. Toast under griller until the cheese is light brown, and cut into fingers to serve.

Makes 6 fingers

Fish fingers

400g / 14oz piece of firm white fish such as flake / cod / sole / hake
Breadcrumbs
Milk
Egg
Olive oil

Cut fish into finger lengths and pat dry with paper towel.
Put breadcrumbs in a bowl, and combine egg and milk in another bowl.
Dip each piece of fish into breadcrumbs, then egg, then breadcrumbs again and shake off excess crumbs. Shallow fry in olive oil until light brown.

Makes 10

Chicken and broccoli pies

The mixture for these pies is the same as that for the gnocchi with chicken and broccoli. Consider making both recipes to save on ingredients.

DIETITIAN'S TIP

Protein is essential for growth and development. Meals and snacks containing protein like egg, meat, cheese or legumes are more filling than those without.

200g / 7oz chicken mince (ground meat)
½ broccoli cut into tiny florets
2 tablespoons / 40g reduced salt tomato paste
Handful grated cheese
2 sheets filo pastry (dough)

Cook broccoli with chicken mince, adding tomato paste and water to avoid sticking. After five minutes, or when chicken is cooked through, stir in grated cheese. Strain mixture to remove excess liquid. Place each sheet of pastry on the benchtop and cut into four, then four again (each sheet makes 16 squares).

Layer four sheets per pie and place some mixture into the middle of each square.

Bring two opposite corners together with a large overlap, and press pastry together. Repeat for the remaining two corners of pastry, ensuring that all four corners overlap. Turn pie over and place on oven tray sprayed with olive oil. Spray the top of each pie with olive oil. Bake at 180°C (355°F) for ten minutes, or until pastry is brown.

Makes 8

healthy baby
snacks

The following section gives many ideas for snacks for babies and toddlers between meals. Make these in bulk, and you will have healthy lasting snacks that will also save you money.

Cereal bars

These bars are great snacks and keep for about a week at room temperature.

2 cups / 125g / 4oz bran or cereal flakes, crushed
1 cup / 100g / 3.5oz rolled (porridge) oats
½ cup / 40g / 1oz shredded coconut
½ cup / 75g / 3oz sultanas
½ cup / 100ml / 3.5fl oz honey
200g / 7oz unsalted butter, melted

DIETITIAN'S TIP

Breakfast is the most important meal of the day. A good breakfast is essential for concentration and school performance, make it a habit right from the start.
On super busy days or while travelling these cereal bars would be a great breakfast alternative.

Combine all ingredients and press firmly into baking tin.
Bake for ten minutes at 170°C (340°F). Cool completely, then slice into bars or squares.

Makes 12

Fruit salad

Fruit salad is easy to make in bulk and keep in an airtight container in the fridge for up to four days, to be served as a healthy nutritious snack or dessert. Give your baby fruit everyday and they will enjoy it into their childhood. Be careful of allergies to kiwifruit in young babies.

3 cups / 450g / 14.5oz chopped fruit:

Selection of banana, kiwifruit, strawberries, apple, rockmelon, honeydew melon, pear, orange, pineapple

Large dollop yoghurt

Combine fruit and yoghurt in a bowl and serve with a fork.

4 serves

Wheat biscuit slice

Wheat biscuits are found in the cereal isle of the supermarket, and can be replaced with any cereal.

5 wheat biscuits, crushed
1 cup / 125g / 4oz self raising flour
1 cup / 80g / 3oz shredded coconut
½ cup / 125g / 4oz sugar
½ cup / 75g / 3oz sultanas
Dash vanilla extract
125g / 4oz butter
1 egg

Mix dry ingredients then add butter, vanilla and egg and mix until well combined. Press into baking tin and cook at 160°C (320°F) for ten minutes or until skewer glides through clean. Slice into pieces.

Makes 16

Ham and corn muffins

The baking paper makes handling the muffins easier, and is optional.

½ cup / 90g / 3oz quick cooking polenta

1 cup / 250ml / 6fl oz milk

3 slices of ham, chopped finely

¼ red onion, finely diced

Handful parsley, chopped

1 cup / 125g / 4oz self raising flour or rice flour (if gluten free)

1 tablespoon / 20g caster sugar

1 cup / 175g / 6oz frozen pea and corn mix

125g / 4oz canned creamed corn

100g / 3.5oz butter, melted

2 eggs

Large handful grated cheese

Baking paper

Cut baking paper into small squares and push into twelve hole mini-muffin pan. Mix polenta and milk, and microwave for twenty seconds, then stir and leave aside. Cook bacon and onion in small pan. Combine flour and sugar in large bowl, stir in corn kernels, creamed corn, polenta and bacon mixture.

Add melted butter and egg, then mix until combined.

Spoon a tablespoon of batter into baking paper in each muffin hole. Bake at 170°C (340°F) for ten minutes.

Makes 20

Date and jam mini-scones

¾ cup / 185ml / 6fl oz milk

¾ cup / 185ml / 6fl oz cream

1 egg, whisked

3 cups / 375g / 12oz self raising flour

1 cup / 150g / 5oz chopped dates

Large dollop strawberry jam

Sift flour, make a well in centre and add egg, milk and cream. Mix until combined and mixture does not stick to sides of bowl. Add dates and strawberry jam and add additional flour if mixture becomes too sticky. Knead dough on a floured surface for a minute, until formed. Push dough down to a two inch layer and cut scones with shaped cutter, or roll into balls and place on baking tray sprayed with olive oil. Bake at 200°C (390°F) for fifteen minutes until golden brown.

Makes 12

Cheese and vegemite pastries

This recipe was developed in Australia. Kids love Vegemite in small amounts. If you prefer use an alternate spread or just cheese.

1 sheet puff pastry
Small amount vegemite
½ cup / 100g / 3.5oz grated cheese
Olive oil spray

Lay defrosted sheet of puff pastry on bench top, spread with vegemite and sprinkle with cheese. Fold pastry in half and cut into small squares. Place onto baking tray sprayed with olive oil spray and bake for ten to fifteen minutes at 180 degrees or until brown. Cool and serve.

Makes 12

Fruit smoothie

DIETITIAN'S TIP

Honey has almost as much sugar as table sugar. However honey has important antibacterial properties, contains very small amounts of vitamins, minerals and phytochemicals. It also has a more complex flavour than sugar and can be used in sweet and savoury dishes.

This recipe will keep in the fridge for two days.

1 cup / 250ml / 8fl oz milk
½ cup / 125ml / 4fl oz yoghurt
½ cup / 75g any fruit
Dash of honey

Combine ingredients in a blender.
Serve in your babies cup, or in an open cup with your help.

2 serves

Banana mini-muffins

75g / 3oz butter

½ cup / 125g / 4oz sugar

2 eggs

2 cups / 250g / 8oz self raising flour

4 tablespoons / 80ml / 3fl oz milk

2 medium sized bananas

Melt butter and combine with all other ingredients.
Combine in mixer or with hand held blender until smooth.
Put into greased mini-muffin tray or patty pans and bake for five to ten minutes
at 170°C (340°F), or until a skewer comes out clean.

Makes 24

Sweet potato chips

This recipe can be used with other vegetables like pumpkin, zucchini, potato and beetroot to make healthy chips.

1 small sweet potato

Olive oil

Pinch salt

Peel potato and slice in to thin discs. Place olive oil into small bowl and coat each slice of potato, removing excess oil on the edge of the bowl. Sprinkle with a tiny amount of salt, and bake at 170°C (340°F), turning over several times, until potato is crispy.

Makes 10

French toast crusts

The bread leftover from this recipe can be used to make braised steak and bread pies.

3 slices bread

1 egg

1 tablespoon / 20ml milk

1 tablespoon / 20g brown sugar

Olive oil

Remove crusts from bread slices and set aside.

Lightly beat egg and add milk and brown sugar.

Soak crusts in egg mix for five minutes, pressing crusts to allow good absorption.

Add a small amount of olive oil to frypan and fry crusts for a minute or two on all sides, or until light brown and crispy.

Makes 12

Wheat cookies

Wheat biscuits are found in the cereal isle of the supermarket, and can be replaced with any cereal.

100g / 3.5oz butter

½ cup / 125g / 4oz sugar

3 crushed wheat biscuits

1 ½ cups / 185g / 6oz self raising flour

1 egg, whisked

Mix butter and sugar together to a soft cream, by beating in a cake mixer for five minutes, or mixing with a wooden spoon for ten minutes. Add egg and remaining ingredients and mix with hands to firm dough. Roll into balls and place on baking tray, with room for the cookies to spread, and bake at 170°C (340°F) for fifteen minutes, or until cookies are light brown.

Makes 12

Rice cereal slice

2 cups / 80g / 3oz rice cereal

½ cup / 60g / 2oz self raising flour

150g / 5oz melted butter

½ cup / 75g / 3oz sultanans

½ cup / 125g / 4oz brown sugar

Combine all ingredients over medium heat in a saucepan for five minutes. Press into a baking tray and refridgerate to set. Cut into squares.

Makes 12

Jam pin-wheels

Use a bread knife when slicing these pin wheels to avoid the uncooked pastry becoming squashed.

1 sheet puff pastry

3 tablespoons / 60g jam

Cut pastry sheet in half and spread

jam across each piece.

Roll each half into a scroll by rolling

one side to the other, lengthwise.

Slice into small discs and put on a

tray lined with baking paper.

Bake at 170°C (340°F) for ten minutes,

or until light brown.

Makes 20

Cheese biscuits

1 cup / 100g / 3.5oz grated cheese

1 cup / 250g / 8oz melted butter

2 cups / 250g / 8oz self raising flour

Mix all ingredients,
then roll into balls and
place on greased baking tray,
spaced apart.
Press down with a fork.
Bake at 170°C (340°F) for
ten minutes,
or until very light brown.

Makes 12

healthy baby
sweeties

Babies can learn from a young age about sweet versus savoury, and the following section gives ideas for low sugar options to follow a savoury course.

Custard and fruit

Making your own custard will save you money and is fresh and nutritious. This recipe contains no added sugar, however you can opt to add sugar or honey. Beware of egg allergies if your baby is under one year old.

3 egg yolks, whisked

1 cup / 250ml / 8fl oz milk, formula or breast milk

3 tablespoons / 60g pureed fruit such as apple or banana

Vanilla extract, optional

Water

Place fruit in the bottom of a small ramekin or oven proof bowl.

Combine eggs, vanilla extract and milk and pour over fruit.

Place ramekin in larger oven proof dish, and pour water half way up the sides of the ramekin (to help the cooking process). Bake at 180°C (350°F) for fifteen minutes, or until the custard is set.

4 serves

Mango rice pudding

This recipe can be used with other fruits such as banana, apple, peaches or pears.

3 tablespoons / 60g fresh or canned mango
½ cup / 125g / 4oz cooked rice
½ cup / 125ml / 4fl oz milk
Dash of honey

Combine all ingredients, warm and serve.

2 serves

Bread and fruit pudding

Use a small ramekin for this recipe, or, double the ingredients and bake in tray of one litre capacity.

2 slices bread
¼ cup / 40g sultanas
2 handfulls dried fruit such as apple and apricot
1 egg
2 tablespoons / 40ml cream
3 tablespoons / 60ml milk
Dash of honey
Sprinkle of brown sugar

Grease ramekin with butter or olive oil. Cut bread slices into triangles, then triangles again, to make eight pieces. Mix egg, milk, cream and honey in small bowl, and combine fruit in separate bowl. Lay bread slices into ramekin, adding fruit between each layer. Pour egg mixture over bread, and press down to remove any excess air. Sprinkle with brown sugar and bake at 170°C (340°F) for twenty minutes, or until the top of the pudding is brown.

4 serves

Fruit crumble

*The fruit used in this recipe can be fresh,
canned or frozen such as banana, pear, apple, peach, berries or apricots.*

¾ cup / 85g / 6oz brown sugar
1 cup / 100g / 3.5oz rolled oats
½ cup / 60g / 2oz plain flour
125g / 4oz butter
2 cups / 300g / 10oz cooked fruit

Place fruit in baking dish.
Combine remaining ingredients and rub together with your hands until the mixture resembles bread crumbs.
Place on top of fruit mix and bake at 170°C (340°F) for twenty minutes, or until brown.

4 serves

DIETITIAN'S TIP

Oats are so nutritious, they are a great source of slowly digested carbohydrates to give kids long lasting energy. Traditional oats are a good source of fibre too.

Strawberry and yoghurt pikelets

You can use other fruit in this recipe such as banana or sultanas.

1 cup / 125g / 4oz plain flour
½ teaspoon / 5g bicarbonate of soda
½ cup / 125g / 4oz plain yoghurt
½ cup / 125ml / 4fl oz milk
1 egg, whisked
1 tablespoon / 20g sugar
8 large strawberries, diced
1 tablespoon / 20g butter

Cook strawberries on low heat for five minutes to soften. Sift flour and bicarbonate of soda, add egg, sugar, milk and yoghurt and stir to a thick batter. Add strawberries and stir to combine. Heat half of the butter in a pan on medium heat, and add tablespoons of the batter. Turn pikelets over when bubbles appear, and cook until slightly brown on both sides.

Makes 16 pikelets

Berry sago

*Sago is a very soft simple texture that young babies love.
The berries can be substituted with banana or other fruits.*

½ cup / 100g / 3.5oz sago
2 cups / 500ml / 16fl oz milk
1 cup / 150g / 6oz
   frozen or fresh berries, pureed

Mix milk and sago,
and leave to soak for five minutes.
Transfer to saucepan and cook
on medium heat for fifteen minutes,
stirring until sago is semi-translucent.
Stir through berries, then pour
into moulds or bowls and
serve immediately, or
allow to set in the fridge.

4 serves

Pineapple pastries

125g / 4oz pineapple pieces
8 sheets filo pastry (dough)
¼ cup / 20g shredded coconut
3 tablespoons / 60g butter

Drain pineapple, then dice and simmer in small pan for five minutes to reduce. Brush each sheet of pastry with melted butter, then cut into half, then half again to make a total of four pieces per pastry sheet. Layer four pieces on top of each other and add a tablespoon of the pineapple, in a line from one corner to the other. Fold the opposing corners into the middle of the pastry, as shown in the photograph. Repeat for the remaining pastry pieces, then brush with butter, sprinkle with coconut and bake at 160°C (330°F) for ten minutes or until brown.

Makes 8

Caramel bananas

3 bananas, sliced
½ cup / 125g / 4oz brown sugar
Dash of cream
3 tablespoons / 60g butter, melted

Place bananas in saucepan. Combine brown sugar, cream and butter in bowl and pour over bananas. Simmer until sauce is thick and bananas are soft.

4 serves

Apple pie

*The sugar syrup in this recipe serves to keep the pie from drying out too much.
You may need to add more of the syrup, depending on the size of your oven dish.*

1 granny smith apple, peeled, cored and quartered

1 sheet shortcrust pastry

1 tablespoon sugar

3 tablespoons water

Quarter pastry sheet, and wrap each quarter around a piece of apple,

sealing by pressing pastry together. Dissolve sugar into water.

Place pies in a small baking tray and pour sugar syrup around the pies,

and place in the oven at 170°C (340°F)

for twenty minutes, or until brown on top.

Makes 4

Stewed rhubarb

Any fruit can be stewed in this way, such as apricots, apples and pears, and babies love cooked fruit with yoghurt, custard, cereal or porridge.

2 cups / 200g / 7oz chopped rhubarb stalks

3 tablespoons / 60ml water

Large dash of honey

DIETITIAN'S TIP

Rhubarb is technically a vegetable but we eat it as a fruit. It is high in fibre and a good source of phosphorous, vitamin A and folate.

Combine ingredients in saucepan and simmer for five minutes, or until stalks are soft. Serve.

4 serves

Banana rice cream

1 ripe banana, mashed

½ cup / 125g / 4oz cooked rice

2 tablespoons / 40ml of cream

Combine and puree, if required, depending on your babies age.

4 serves

Baked apples with yoghurt

*The apple peel does soften once cooked,
however, you may wish to peel the apples if your baby is very young.*

3 apples, cored and sliced into bite size pieces, skin on
½ cup / 75g / 2.5oz sultanas
Dash of honey
3 tablespoons / 60ml plain yoghurt

Combine all ingredients in a baking dish and bake at 170°C (340°F) for thirty minutes, or until apple is soft.

4 serves

sweeties

healthy baby

fussy eaters

fussy eaters

The best research in this area recommends that a Division of Responsibility is established around eating. That is the parents decide what, when and where to feed children, and the child determines how much and whether or not to eat. It is important that you avoid pressuring or bribing your child to eat.

Do not be offended if your baby decides to reject the food you have prepared - take a deep breath and press on, this is completely normal. There are a myriad of reasons why babies become fussy, and once these reasons are understood, you can try your best to overcome them. It is important to know though, that on occasion, you may try everything, and your baby still refuses to eat. At this time, remember the Division of Responsibility and take another deep breath! Keep persevering with the ideas below and this should pass. If you are concerned, consult your doctor or health care nurse. The following section provides some explanations and suggested solutions to the common reasons for fussy eating.

Sleep

Babies are difficult to manage when they are overtired. As a carer or parent, your tolerance level will be very low when you are sleep deprived, and the two in combination can be very stressful. Fussy eating is often linked with sleep problems, and it is worth taking some time to invest in good sleep for you and your baby. Not only will this help them eat better, it also helps their general growth and develop and their ability to learn new things. With the exception of rare medical conditions, it is usually possible to get babies sleeping through the night, and there are resources available to help such as books, health care providers and websites.

Independence

When babies are small, they enjoy being spoon fed mushy food by you at meal times. Once they reach a certain age, they become more independent, and may refuse the spoon held by you, and this is sometimes confused with fussy eating. They start to notice that adults don't eat mushy food, and will become interested in more advanced foods. At this time, try finger foods, and also hand over the fork or spoon to them. The finger foods section of this book has many ideas such as the pasta cakes, toast ideas and pea and corn fritters that are soft and easy to hold. Also try giving your baby a fork or spoon and letting them bring the food to their mouth. They may need help initially, but once they get the hang of it you wont be able to get the fork out of their hands! Pasta and gnocchi are great for learning initial fork skills and thick soup is great for using a spoon. Be assured that the amount of mess does decrease as their skills improve!

Flavour

As your child experiences more sugary and salty foods as they get older, they may seem to reject the plainer, blander foods they previously enjoyed. Don't despair, more flavour does not have to mean adding more salt or sugar. Rather than flavouring normally bland foods like avocado, potato or porridge, serve them with more strongly flavoured foods, and this way your child will still eat their old favourites.

Boredom

As your baby develops, he or she will need more stimulation at meal times. Your baby may refuse to eat because they find the experience monotonous and boring.

The line "here comes the airplane" didn't come from nowhere. Keep mealtimes as fun as possible by incorporating play and giving them your attention. Always remember that a healthy baby will eat when they are hungry.

Try varying the routine by feeding your baby in a different location - try feeding on your lap or propped up with pillows or sitting on the floor. Let someone else feed them, sometimes your baby will take food from grandparents or friends and not from you.

Stress

Babies will feel the stress in their environment, and although challenging, you must try your best to make mealtimes as relaxed as possible. Be aware of your facial expressions, your tone of voice, and general manner. Engage with your baby, explaining the names of the vegetables and other food names and provide positive affirmation when they are eating well, such as clapping, smiling and hugging. This is challenging I know, but do your best!

Sore Teeth

Occassionally, teething can put babies off their food, particularly when several teeth come through at once. This may be observed as refusal to chew, sucking food for a long time, and crying when chewing. If you observe these things, try giving your baby soft foods such as scrambled eggs, boston beans and cooked fruit and yoghurt.

Illness

Like adults, babies can become fussy eaters when they are not feeling well. During these eary years, their immune systems are being bombarded with germs, and they will need extra attention to keep up their food intake when they are sick. At this time, they may only feel simple foods such as toast, fruit and yoghurt or a fruit smoothie.

Vegetables

Babies can sometimes refuse to eat vegetables, and it is worth challenging them early on this one, as it is harder to change, the older they get. As mentioned at the beginning of this book, vegetables help babies grow and develop to their full potential and also assist their immune systems to fight diseases. It is a good idea make vegetables part of every meal, and for babies to see their parents, grandparents and other significant people in their lives eating vegetables. Once your baby can hold finger food, you may want to keep a container of chopped and steamed vegetables in your fridge to be given out as snacks and at the start of each meal.

Ideas to make vegetables more popular include:

- Use a vegetable peeler and make thin strips of carrot and cucumber
- Stir fry vegetables with or without meat
- Grate and chop vegetables into fritters, patties, frittatas, omelettes and quiche to vary texture and flavour
- Add some grated vegetables to pasta sauces such as macaroni cheese and bolognese
- Once your baby can chew uncooked vegetables, give them small pieces of chopped vegetables such as carrot and capsicum
- Recipes such as roast vegetable medley and pasta with vegetable sauce

The Buffet

You may want to give your baby a selection of foods in the one meal, if they start to refuse one course. Although challenging, keep presenting your baby with varied food options when they are going through a fussy stage, either on the one plate, or one course after the other. Try preparing

several meal options and keeping them in the fridge, then warm through as needed for up to four days.

Examples include:

1. Beef rissoles, steamed carrot and broccoli, cheese and boiled egg on the one plate.
2. Pork and vegetable stirfry followed by raisin toast and yoghurt.
3. Chicken and vegetable soup followed by scrambled tomato eggs, fruit and yoghurt.
4. Tuna pasta bake followed by berry sago.
5. Roast vegetable medley followed by tuna patties.

It is worth persevering to ensure your baby has a full belly before bedtime, to increase the chances of a good nights sleep.

I hope that some of these ideas alleviate the frustration that can be associated with fussy eating, and that your baby continues to eat a wide range of nutritious food.

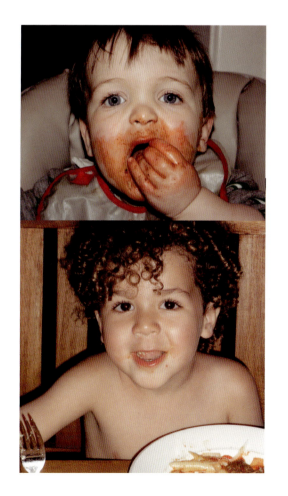

index

healthy baby

A

Apricots
   Chicken rice   56.
   In bread and butter pudding   134.

Apple
   Baked with yoghurt   143.
   Pie   140.
   Puree   26.
   With rice cereal   26.

Aubergine (see eggplant)

Avocado
   In Cous Cous salad   43.
   Puree   27.

B

Bacon
   And banana toast   111.
   In slow cook with chicken   83.

Banana
   And bacon toast   111.
   Caramel   139.
   Mini-muffins   123.
   Puree   27.
   Rice cream   142.

Beans
   And pumpkin squares   106.
   Boston (baked) beans   57.
   In mexican wraps   86.

Beef
   Rissoles   105.
   Stroganoff   85.
   With spinach   41.
   With sweet potato   38.

Bolognese
   First   39.
   Second   47.

Braised steak and bread pies   79.

Bread
   French Toast crusts   125.
   Fruit pudding   134.
   Toast ideas   108.
   Sandwich ideas   89.
   Steak and bread pies   79.

Broccoli
   Gnocchi with chicken   50.
   Pies with chicken   113.
   Puree   29.

C

Cereal
  Bars 116.
  Slice 127.

Cheesey macaroni 63.

Cheese
  And vegemite pastries 121.
  Biscuits 130.
  Cheesey macaroni 63.
  Spinach and cheese pie 90.

Chicken
  And bacon slow cook 83.
  And broccoli pies 113.
  And corn 34.
  And mushroom quiche 65.
  And pea risotto 68.
  With red lentils and pasta 22.
  And vegetable cous cous 78.
  And vegetable scrolls 73.
  And vegetable soup 103.
  Croquettes 81.
  Pasta bake 56.
  With apricots and rice 42.
  With hokkien noodles and vegetables 84.
  With broccoli and gnocchi 50.
  With corn 34.

Corn
  And ham muffins 119.
  And pea fritters 110.
  With chicken 34.
  In Cous Cous salad 43.
  In mexican wraps 86.
  In vegetable lasagne 53.
  With pumpkin and gnocchi 51.

Courgette (see zucchini)

Cous Cous
  Salad 43.
  With chicken and vegetables 78.
  With eggplant and sweet potato 44.
  With pumpkin and yoghurt 33.

Custard
  With fruit 132.

D

Date and jam mini-scones 120.

E

Egg
- In Cous Cous salad — 43.
- On toast — 108.
- Scrambled with ricotta and parsely — 48.
- With breadcrumbs — 54.
- Scrambled tomato — 69.
- With breadcrumbs — 54.
- With fried rice — 67.

Eggplant (Aubergine)
- With sweet potato and cous cous — 44.

F

Fish
- Fingers — 112.
- With vegetables — 75.

Flat bread toasties — 95.
French toast crusts — 125.
Fried rice with egg — 67.
Fruit
- Crumble — 135.
- Salad — 117.
- Smoothie — 122.

G

Gnocchi
- With broccoli and chicken — 50.
- With pumpkin and corn — 51.

H

Ham
- And corn muffins — 119.
- And polenta squares — 109.
- And vegetable fritatta — 55.
- And vegetable ratatouille — 59.
- And vegetable slice — 100.
- And zucchini soup — 76.
- With lentils — 60.
- With vegetables and rice — 49.

Hokkein noodles with chicken and vegetables — 42.

J

Jam
- And date mini-scones — 120.
- Pin-wheels — 129.

L

Lamb
Patties 94.
Skewers 92.

Lasagne
With meat 72.
With vegetables 53.

Lentils
Puree 29.
With chicken and pasta 36.
With ham 60.
With vegetables and pasta 35.

M

Mango
Rice pudding 133.

Mexican wraps 86.

Mince (ground) meat
In meatballs 80.
In pasta bolognese 39. & 47.
In lasagne 72.
In sheperds pie 66.
In rissoles 105.

Muffins
Banana mini 123.
Ham and corn 119.

Mushrooms
In quiche with chicken 65.

N

Noodles
Hokkein noodles with chicken and vegetables 42.
Rice noodles with chicken and vegetables 84.

P

Pasta
Cakes 91.
Cheesey macaroni 63.
Chicken pasta bake 81.
In pasta bolognese 39. & 47.
Tuna pasta bake 77.
With chicken and lentils 36.
With lentils and vegetables 35.
With pork 70.
With sausages 61.
With vegetable sauce 58.

Pasty slice 96.

Peas
And corn fritters 110.
In fried rice 67.
In risotto with chicken 68.

Pikeletes
   Strawberry and yoghurt   136.
Pineapple
   In sweet and sour pork   74.
   Pastries   138.
Pizza   97.
Polenta
   And ham squares   109.
   With vegetables   40.
Pork
   Roast with gravy   71.
   Sweet and sour   74.
   With pasta   70.
Potato
   And leek soup   82.
   In chicken croquettes   22.
Pumpkin
   Puree   28.
   And bean squares   106.
   With rice cereal   28.
   And cheese balls   101.
   Gnocchi with corn   51.
   In vegetables lasagne   53.
   With Cous Cous and yoghurt   33.

Q
Quiche
   Alternate fillings   65.
   Chicken and mushroom   65.

R
Rhubarb
   Stewed   141.
Rice
   Chicken and pea risotto   68.
   Fried with egg   22.
   In Mexican wraps   22.
   With apricots and chicken   56.
   With ham and vegetables   49.
   With sweet potato   37.
Roast vegetable medley   102.

S
Sago
   Berry sago   137.
Sandwich ideas   89.
Sausages
   And pasta   61.
Schnitzel fingers   107.
Scones
   Date and jam   120.
Sheperds Pie   66.

Spinach	
And cheese pie	90.
With beef	41.
Spring rolls	95.
Strawberry	
And yoghurt pikelets	136.
Berry sago	137.
Sweet potato	
Chips	124.
With eggplant and cous cous	44.
With beef	38.
With rice	37.

T

Toast ideas	108.
Tuna	
Pasta bake	77.
Patties	104.

V

Vegetables	
And chicken with cous cous	78.
And chicken scrolls	93.
And ham and rice	49.
And ham frittata	55.
And ham slice	100.
Chicken and vegetable scrolls	99.
Chicken and vegetable soup	73.
In pasta sauce	58.
In sweet and sour pork	22.
Lasagne	53.
Roasted medley	102.
With chicken and hokkein noodles	42.
With fish	75.
With ham in ratatouille	59.
With lentils and pasta	35.
And polenta	40.

W

Wheat biscuits	
In biscuits	126.
In slice	118.

Z

Zucchini	
And ham soup	76.
In fritatta	55.
In Mexican wraps	86.
In pasta with pork	70.

First published in Australia in 2010 by

New Holland Publishers (Australia) Pty Ltd

Sydney • Auckland • London • Cape Town

1/66 Gibbes Street Chatswood NSW 2067 Australia

218 Lake Road Northcote Auckland New Zealand

86 Edgware Road London W2 2EA United Kingdom

80 McKenzie Street Cape Town 8001 South Africa

Copyright © 2010 New Holland Publishers (Australia) Pty Ltd

Copyright © 2010 text and photographs Nirelle Tolstoshev

All rights reserved. No part of this publication may be reproduced, stored in a retrieval system or transmitted, in any form or by any means, electronic, mechanical, photocopying, recording or otherwise, without the prior written permission of the publishers and copyright holders.

A record of this book is held at the National Library of Australia

ISBN 9781742570334

Publisher: Fiona Schultz

Publishing Manager: Lliane Clarke

Designer: Ben Tolstoshev

Photographs: Ben & Nirelle Tolstoshev

Food stylist: Ben & Nirelle Tolstoshev

Production Manager: Olga Dementiev

Printed By: Toppan Leefung Printing Ltd. (China)

10 9 8 7 6 5 4 3 2 1